THE B
TO DO EVERYTHING

THE BEST TIME
TO DO EVERYTHING:

EXPERT ADVICE ON HOW TO LIVE COOLER,
SMARTER, FASTER, BETTER

MICHAEL KAPLAN

BLOOMSBURY

Published by Bloomsbury Publishing, New York and London
Distributed to the trade by Holtzbrinck Publishers

All papers used by Bloomsbury Publishing are natural, recyclable
products made from wood grown in well-managed forests.
The manufacturing processes conform to the environmental
regulations of the country of origin.

Library of Congress Cataloging-in-Publication Data

Kaplan, Michael, 1959–
The best time to do everything : expert advice on how to live
cooler, smarter, faster, better / Michael Kaplan.—1st U.S. ed.
p. cm.
ISBN 1-58234-487-6 (pbk.)
1. Conduct of life. 2. Life skills. I. Title.
BJ1595.K296 2004
646.7—dc22
2004014827

ISBN-13 9781582344874

First U.S. Edition 2005

1 3 5 7 9 10 8 6 4 2

Typeset by Palimpsest Book Production Limited,
Polmont, Stirlingshire, Scotland
Printed in the United States of America
by Quebecor World Fairfield

For Melodie, Lola, and Chloe

In February of 2000, my wife and I sold our Manhattan apartment. New York real estate being what it is, we made a healthy profit. Four months later, in June, we took that money and put it toward a lovely brownstone in Brooklyn. We paid a decent price, and I felt pretty good about both deals.

Then I happened to speak with a real estate broker who challenged the logic of my timing. "Housing prices are lowest in winter," he stated. "And they're highest in summer." That means, relatively speaking, I sold low and bought high.

"It's a matter of supply and demand," the realtor explained. "More people are looking to buy houses in the spring and summer. That's when prices rise. Then, because fewer people want to move during cold-weather months, prices drop in the winter. Simple."

Oh. It got me to thinking about how much I could have saved by timing things a little differently. Then I began considering all the other things that could be timed more effectively: buying shoes, making restaurant reservations, finding a job, playing basketball, getting married, saving for retirement. How great would it be to know the best time to do everything? Especially if you could go to impeccable sources for the information: Donald Trump on the best time to haggle, punk-rock star Johnny Ramone on the best time to learn guitar, mob lawyer Bruce Cutler on the best time to plead the Fifth, Bill Maher on the best time to talk politics, David Blaine on the best time to do magic.

So I set out to find all the answers, conducting nearly two hundred interviews with some of the best minds on every subject from gaming to romance to cooking to travel to—yes—real estate. Follow the advice within these pages and you'll be able to make your life cooler, smarter, faster, better, and much more efficient. Plus, if someone happens to ask you when might be the best time to run into a burning building, how you can get your hands on the freshest fish, or when to snag a hotel-room upgrade, you'll have the answers.

THE BEST TIME
TO DO EVERYTHING

Best Time to Buy a New Car

Auto prices are always somewhat negotiable, but at the end of every month, salesmen become downright flexible. It's when they focus more on volume and less on commissions from individual car sales. "We have monthly quotas that we try to hit," says Fred Altman, one of America's most successful Dodge salesmen (he works out of Christopher's Dodge World in Golden, Colorado, which consistently ranks among the country's top dealerships). "Everything in the car business is on a monthly schedule. Sell enough cars in a given month and you get a higher commission percentage the next month, as well as a better work schedule. As the thirtieth and thirty-first approach, I am definitely more aggressive in closing sales."

Best Time to Launch
a High-Fashion Modeling Career

You see those pale-skinned beauties flaunting string-bean physiques, strutting down catwalks, and figure you can do it, too. Hopefully, this decision is being reached before you're old enough to drive. "For a woman, the best time to start exploring a modeling career is when she is a junior in high school," says Michael Flutie, who co-owns Flutie Entertainment and once managed the likes of Cindy Crawford, Elle McPherson, and James King.

"It's a year prior to graduation, and she'll have time to explore the possibilities. Before becoming a full-time model, though, a girl wants to be finished with high school. After graduation, she should plan on spending the twelve months one would ordinarily devote to freshman year of college in trying out the business. If a girl waits till after she's done with college, she's too old. And if she tries doing it at fourteen, the industry will love her, but mistakes get made when a young teenager is standing in front of the camera and exuding sex for a fifty-year-old male photographer. Young girls get drawn in and don't have what it takes, emotionally, to deal with the industry."

Men who want to enter modeling have it easier, at least in terms of the timing: "For men, it should be right after college or else during sophomore or junior year. Women need to look like girls, but male models should look like men."

Best Time for a First Kiss

Em and Lo (aka Emma Taylor and Lorelei Sharkey), tag-team sex columnists and authors of *The Big Bang*, suggest ditching the clichéd end-of-first-date lip lock and thinking outside the box: middle of the second date. "After the first date," they opine, "you might not even know whether or not the other person really likes you, and you have a chance of getting the cheek instead of the lips"—a depressing denouement. "But by the second date, he or she is obviously interested, and by not waiting until the end of that date, you break the ice and get any lingering tension out of the way." But what if your date seems immediately and totally into you? Does that make your first night out together suitable for a smooch? Uh-uh. "There is something cool about delayed gratification, which can be very sexy."

Best Time to Teach Your Dog a Trick

Remember the movie *Gladiator*? It contains a stunning scene in which the character played by Russell Crowe gets pawed and clawed by an angry tiger. Not surprisingly, that wasn't Crowe under the big cat. More surprisingly, the attack was done without special effects. Randy Miller, Hollywood's reigning master of the wild animal–attack scene, got mauled for real, and Crowe's face was digitally implanted later on. While Miller, a trainer of ferocious beasts, lives in a Northern California compound with his lions and tigers and bears, he also has a handful of dogs, which are among the most disciplined you'll ever meet.

He says that the best time to teach your dog a trick is soon after the canine's first birthday. "The dog's young and active, but maturing quickly, and his brain is developing," says Miller. "On the other hand, he's not so young that he can't understand what you want him to do. To *sit* and *stay* are the first things you need to teach a dog, as those are both required for him to behave in a reasonable manner when he's around people or other animals. Next you train him to come to you when you call. Get those down, and then after that, he can learn to do the fun stuff: play dead, or shake hands, or roll over."

🕐 *Purebred Cheat Sheet* 🕐

Before you train your dog, you'll need to select the right one. Here are five popular breeds of dog and what you can expect from them, according to details provided by the American Kennel Club.

Akita: This breed originated in Japan and was first brought to the United States by Helen Keller. These are large, muscular dogs, said to be good with kids but standoffish with strangers. They require a fenced yard (in other words, don't keep an Akita confined in your apartment).

Bichon frise: Not surprisingly, this handbag-size pooch is a favorite with the "ladies who lunch" set. This dog requires lots of pampering, enjoys sitting in its owner's lap, and has a coat that needs to be frequently brushed. On the positive side, the bichon has a generally upbeat disposition.

Boxer: This breed is appropriately named, as boxers strike with a front paw when fighting. These well-built dogs can do guard work, but they have mild enough temperaments to provide companionship as well.

Fox terrier: Strong and compact, they were originally bred for hunting foxes and badgers. These dogs are surprisingly powerful—especially in light of their petite size—and can be gratingly high-strung.

Siberian husky: This is a terrific dog if you need to win a four-hundred-mile sled race (in 1910, John "Iron Man" Johnson brought acclaim to the breed after acing such an event, traveling through the wilds of Alaska with a pack of huskies pulling him). The American Kennel Club warns that huskies "shed nonstop" and "must be kept under control at all times." But before you turn your back on this native of Siberia, consider that the AKC also describes the Siberian husky as a "friendly and gentle dog [that] makes a wonderful companion." Mush!

Best Time to Buy Shoes

In the afternoon. "You want to wait until you've been walking around for a while and your feet have swelled a bit," says Dr. Bruce R. Saferin, a Toledo, Ohio–based podiatrist who serves on the board of the American Podiatric Medical Association. "Buy shoes on your way to work in the morning, and by the afternoon, you'll wonder why they're hurting your feet. In case the shoes you buy in the afternoon feel a little loose in the morning, don't worry. Your feet will spread out once you start walking around."

Best Time to Place a Sports Bet

"If you're looking to play the underdog, wait till game time; if you want to play a favorite, then you probably should jump on it as early as you can," says Keith Glantz, former professional sports bettor and current line maker for the Associated Press.

The reason for this is that most amateur bettors wager on favorites, and they tend to place their bets close to game time. Because bookies are getting lots of wagers on favorites during those pregame minutes, they move the point spread to attract action to the underdogs. Their goal here is to achieve something close to a balance of bets on both sides (bookies make money by charging a 10 percent betting commission, or vigorish). "Generally speaking," adds Glantz, "there is more value in the underdog than there is in the favorite. That's why smart gamblers just sit there, watch the point spread move in the 'dog's favor, and wait till it makes a nice jump before betting." What if you place one bet and it moves further in your favor? "By all means, bet again. And again."

Best Time to Haggle

Whether he's buying a Manhattan skyscraper or a pair of Manolo Blahniks for his beloved, Donald Trump likes to haggle. And he advises that the best time to do it is when you are willing to walk away from the deal—with no remorse. "You can negotiate any price in any store," says Trump. "You can negotiate with jewelry stores and all the dress companies in Manhattan."

Does he ever get self-conscious? "It is a little embarrassing for me because I'm Trump," he admits. "But I always get something taken off the asking price. Any woman who pays full price for a dress is wasting her boyfriend's and/or her husband's money." How does he do it? "I go into a place, see something that's selling for ten thousand dollars, and say, 'I'll give you two thousand for that.' They might not sell it to me for two thousand, but I'll get it for five thousand, which is still half the price. Remember, though, that your only leverage is a willingness to say, 'Forget it.' If you're not up for leaving the store empty-handed, salespeople will insist that they can't go below the list price. Walk away a couple times and see how fast they reduce the price for you in the future."

Best Time to Buy Art

You might think that the best time to buy art would be when a painting or sculpture really speaks to you. And to an extent, that is true. But that alone is also a sure road to financial ruin if you hope to cash out one day.

Craig Robins, a Miami real estate developer and art patron with a collection in excess of six hundred modern works, suggests a business-oriented approach. "The best time to buy art is when there is a big gap between the primary market [that is, buying directly from the artist's dealer] and the secondary market [buying from individuals who are selling pieces that they've owned for a while, usually at auction, but sometimes through a dealer]," says Robins, pointing out that art bought from a primary source is usually 20 to 30 percent cheaper than art bought from a secondary source.

"The other good time is during a moment when artists who are very clearly a part of our history are not being hyped. Sometimes the market gets fixated on young, less proven, more open-ended artists, whose contributions to the future of art are in question." That's the time to pounce on the older guys, whose prices are taking temporary dips even as they produce work that will clearly be coveted by collectors and curators in the long run. It's sort of like buying stock in Exxon when everybody else seems focused on bloated offerings like Ariba. (Remember that one? It rose to more than one hundred dollars per share before plummeting to zero in less than three years.)

☺ *Art Appreciation Class* ☺

On January 22, 2004, the *Wall Street Journal* ran an article that tracked the growth and depreciation of various artworks. The story proved that if you buy wisely, you can definitely make as much money with art as you can in the stock market. Invest in the wrong pieces, however, and you have the graphic equivalent of Enron to contend with. Here's how, according to the *Journal,* a few hot and cold artists have fared over the years.

Keith Haring (famous for his radiant babies, which began as chalk sketches inside vacant black sign frames in New York City subway stations): increased by 300 percent over the last fifteen years; record auction price is $402,000.

Damien Hirst (creates pieces that consist of graphically interesting pills and builds sculptures composed of large animals—chopped in half, floating in formaldehyde; favored artist of famed adman/collector Charles Saatchi): increased by 131 percent over the last five years; record auction price is $1.2 million.

Jeff Koons (stockbroker turned creator of kitschy collectibles, including a giant sculpture of Michael Jackson alongside his chimp, Bubbles, and super-realistic paintings of Koons having sex with Italian porn star and ex-wife Ilona Cicciolina): increased by 1,786 percent over the last fifteen years; record auction price is $5.6 million.

Juilian Schnabel (former restaurant chef and current film director, extremely cocky; has augmented paintings with cracked dinner plates—pieces were notorious for falling apart): decreased by 39 percent over the last fifteen years; record auction price is $361,500.

Andy Warhol (granddaddy of Pop Art, famous for portraits of Marilyn, Mick, and the Campbell's soup can): decreased by 28 percent over the last five years, after increasing by 39 percent in the preceding fifteen years; record auction price is $17.3 million.

Best Time to Buy Tickets from a Scalper

The absolute best time is when a seemingly sold-out event suddenly isn't exactly sold out anymore. "The promoters hate us," says a fellow we'll call George Valdez, leader of a gang of Mexican ticket scalpers in Southern California. "Sometimes they'll hold back a bunch of tickets and put them on sale at the last minute, maybe an hour before a concert that's been sold out for months. Once that happens, we're screwed and our ticket prices plummet. Same thing when they suddenly add a second or third show after one or two have completely sold out."

If nothing beyond the scalper's control works in your favor, wait until it's a few minutes before game time or halfway through the opening act's set. "Ticket hustlers like to make you think that if you don't buy a ticket immediately, you'll never get in—or you'll never get a decent seat—and that's just not true," admits George. "Good seats pop up all the time, not just an hour or two before the event. And at a certain point, the tickets become completely worthless. We'll literally rip them up and throw them in the trash—or sell them for less than face value. It's all about supply and demand, and, for many events, there are more tickets out there than there are people willing to pay a premium."

Best Time to Work Out

Weight training can be done at any time of the day, with no adverse consequences or benefits, but, according to Michael Hewitt, research director for exercise science at Canyon Ranch Spa, morning is the best time for cardio-vascular workouts. "Cardiovascular exercise requires a considerable amount of blood flow to the tissues, and you don't want any of your body's blood to be used for digestion at that time," he says. "So we advise exercising before eating a moderate to large breakfast. Beyond that, your metabolic rate drops when you sleep, and exercising first thing in the morning bumps it up. Throughout the day, your metabolism will run slightly higher if you exercise in the morning."

Best Time to Chuck It All and Set Sail

When you reach your mid- to late forties. So says Melodye Pompa, who maintains the Web site caribcruisers.com and, along with her husband, cashed out of the tech industry to hit the open seas in 1993.

Beyond your age, she advises, you need to wait until you've got enough money to walk away from full-time work and are emotionally prepared to stop achieving in the conventional sense. The idea is that by your late forties, you will have accumulated substantial savings and made a big mark in your profession. "Plus, you need to be physically able to live at sea," says Pompa, now in her late fifties, who sold three cars and a house in New England before taking off. "It requires a lot of strength to get out of hairy situations—storms and such—in the middle of the ocean. It's not all rum punch on the beach all the time. We lost our pump yesterday, and that was not a lot of fun."

While Pompa says that she'd want no other life, she acknowledges "feeling like I have a lot less energy than I did ten years ago." She also warns that there is a relatively small window for all of this: "By the time most of our friends are in their mid-sixties, they're getting to the point where they want to call it quits. So you need to do it as soon as you reach that moment when money and energy levels converge. If you keep waiting for more money and more money and more money, you will never do it."

Best Time to Buy the Arcade Game of Your Youth

Most people—okay, most guys—have fond college memories of banging around on pinball machines and video games when they should have been studying sociology. Larry DeMar, who has developed important pinball machines (Addams Family, High Speed) and video games

(Defender, Robotron) had his share of arcade obsessions, and he now keeps thirty or so machines in the basement of his Chicago home. So he should be able to nail the timing of this one.

DeMar suggests that the best time to buy an arcade game is ten years after you graduate from college. "That puts you in your early thirties," he explains. "You've got the money to pay for it"—anticipate spending between one thousand and four thousand dollars for a machine in good condition—"and the space to keep it, your reflexes are still suitably sharp that you'll be able to play well, and enough time has passed for the nostalgia factor to kick in."

Just as importantly, there is the cost angle. "The life cycle of an arcade game being a moneymaker is something like ten years," DeMar continues. "Chances are that the machine you enjoyed playing in college will no longer be hot enough to generate much revenue ten years later—and it won't be old enough to be considered an antique. That way, you'll be able to get the machine for a decent price"—say closer to one thousand dollars than four thousand.

⏱ *The Amazing Secrets of MAME* ⏱

Want to turn your computer into a giant arcade? It's easy, it's online, and you won't need to send a certified check to a post office box in Terre Haute, Indiana. Run by a shadowy cartel of gaming fanatics, MAME (it stands for Multiple Arcade Machine

Emulator) offers downloadable programs, free of charge, for just about every video game that's ever been created.

Go to its site (www.mame.net), download the programs, outfit your laptop with a joystick, and relive your youth. If you really want to go crazy, go to google.com and do a search for "MAME, cabinets." You'll find links to sites that sell kits for building wood-grain boxes that duplicate the machines that used to eat your lunch money. "Then it's totally like having the *original machine*," enthuses DeMar, who doesn't mind one bit that his games are up there and free for the grabbing. "It's just awesome."

Best Time to Take a Chance in Business

For a Las Vegas hotelier, George Maloof had it made: His Fiesta Casino thrived as a gambling magnet for locals, and the place generated a fortune for Maloof. But it wasn't the kind of happening operation that would turn up every week on MTV's *Real World* or draw the likes of Kid Rock and Pamela Anderson and a bevy of *Playboy* Playmates. So he sold his sure thing for $185 million and used that money to take a chance on building a far hipper gambling den, the Palms. Since its grand opening in 2001, the Palms has been the hottest joint in town (and the setting for a season of *The Real World*, not to mention a prime destination for Pam and Kid and the Playmates).

What made the time right for such a high-risk maneuver? "The market desperately needed what I had to offer," Maloof says of the cool and boutiquey Palms. "Everybody had built mega–theme resorts on the Vegas Strip. I was going to put up something more intimate, and I knew there were people who wanted it." The idea here is that the best time to take a chance is when it has a high probability of paying off because you are filling a wide-open chasm of need.

Maloof also points out, however, that the best time to take a chance has an expiration date. He figures it's before your fortieth birthday. "When you take a huge risk—and for me it was massive; I put all $185 million of my money into the Palms—you'd better have the time and energy to make it work out. I'm about to turn forty, and I can guarantee that I'll never again do anything like this with my own money."

Best Time to Buy Designer Clothing

January and February are the months when you will get the best prices for winter wear. Spring lines get deeply discounted after July Fourth, though prices begin going down on Father's Day. "But even if you wait until July, you'll still get plenty of summer use out of the clothing," says Ken Seiff, founder of bluefly.com, an on-line discounter of designer garments, where prices are routinely 40 to 70 percent off of the retail price. "Same idea with winter clothes, since, these days, cold weather doesn't really kick in until after the first of the year."

If you can't wait to start saving, Seiff advises that the Thanksgiving weekend is as early as you want to begin shopping. "That's when the clearance racks first emerge, and the stores begin correcting their mistakes"—by dumping out clothing that won't sell at retail prices. "The selection is good, and you will get a longer season of wear, but the prices continue to fall until January or February."

Another good time to buy designer clothing is the night before a sale. Though this is not a hard-and-fast rule, there have been plenty of incidents of people showing up, selecting clothing, and paying the markdown price without having to contend with crowds and diminishing stock.

Best Time to Argue Your Case

When the bigger picture is in your favor. For instance, if you're a fifteen-year-old trying to convince your parents that there's nothing wrong with your hanging out at Snoop Dogg's house, the time to do it is on the day that he and his posse have gotten some kind of a civic award (maybe for redefining ebonics—*fo' shizzle*), not after they've been busted for driving around with guns and chronic. Similar thinking applies if you're arguing for a raise at your job or debating constitutional rights regarding the privacy of defendants. "The best time for that is now"—if you want the defendants to have fewer rights—says Carter G. Phillips, a Washington, D.C.–based attorney who specializes in presenting Supreme Court arguments. "Since September 11, the government's prerogatives have changed, and you'll be riding the tide, rather than swimming against it."

In court, and in life, Phillips says, he tries to time his arguments for the days when outside factors will help things along. "If you want to benefit from a quick decision in the Supreme Court," he says, "you will try to plead your case in April. Justices need to have their opinions written by June, so they'll resolve things quickly. But if you start in October, then they have all the time in the world to consider it. You have to remember that three out of four cases heard by the Supreme Court get reversed. If you are the petitioner"—that is, the person trying to get a charge turned around—"and you come in with just a little time left, things are even more in your favor."

Best Time to Paint Walls and Refinish Wooden Floors

"Ideally, it's before you move in," says Jeff Wilson, host of *Blueprint for Homebuilding* on cable TV's DIY Network and an inveterate do-it-yourselfer. "You save a lot of money by not paying people to move furniture for you." Failing that, it's best to have the floors done when you won't be around. "Volatile compounds are used to strip wood, and the stink is awful."

In considering the time of year—to paint and refinish—aim for a period when humidity is at its lowest. "Floors and walls dry quicker then, and there will be fewer opportunities for bugs and dust particles to settle in and rough up the smoothness."

If you want to schedule both jobs together, do the floors first, give them a chance to dry, wait for the dust to settle, and then work on painting the walls. "It's easy to cover up floors," says Wilson. "But it's hard to deal with dust. You get that stuff on freshly painted walls and it's difficult to clean off—especially if the walls are not completely dry."

One more tip from Wilson: "If you want to protect your floors, insist that visitors take their shoes off before coming into your home. It does more than just keep a place clean. Grit hurts floors. It gets ground in and wears down the finish."

✪ *Wood Floors Cheat Sheet* ✪

All woods are not created equal. Here is Jeff Wilson's guide to the ones that look cool, wear well, and bend to your designerly whims.

Pine

Characteristics: wide-grain wood, typically light in color; a step up from standard pine is southern yellow pine, which is a bit more resilient.

Pros: inexpensive, absorbs stain well, easy to install because it's soft.

Cons: Due to its softness, pine develops more dings over time. Drop a heavy pan on a pine floor and you will see a dent.

Oak

Characteristics: close-grain wood, may have a slightly salmon-colored tint, greatly varies in terms of pattern (which compensates for the wood's ubiquity).

Pros: hard and sturdy, lots of choices in terms of shading and width, very common and easy to find, inexpensive because a lot of people use it and it is widely available.

Cons: easy to split when you hammer in nails during installation; so many people choose oak, your floors will look just like your neighbors'.

Maple

Characteristics: tight-grain wood, hard, lightly colored, has appealingly wavy patterns.

Pros: looks modern, very resilient.

Cons: more difficult to find than oak, expensive, doesn't take stain as well as pine or oak.

Bamboo

Characteristics: Fairly tight-grain wood, consistent patterns.

Pros: absolutely beautiful and unique, looks exotic, an ecologically responsible choice because it replenishes easily.

Cons: tends to wear out quickly, can be difficult to find, will break your budget.

Teak

Characteristics: tight-grain wood, hard, a dark color, doesn't need stain.

Pros: many times harder than oak, very resilient, unique-looking, oily enough that even in an unfinished state it is unlikely to get scratched.

Cons: so hard that if you want to work with it, you will need to use a drill—along with a hammer—to avoid splitting wood and bending nails, pricey, an ecologically irresponsible choice because it comes out of the Indonesian rain forest and the continual harvesting of teak trees is slowly destroying the forest.

Best Time to Cheat on Your Diet

This depends on what kind of cheating you want to do. If it's a pit stop for a XXL fat feast at Burger King, do your exercises fifteen to seventeen hours before chowing down. "It takes that long for the enzymes, which will clear fat from your blood—and are most efficient after exercising—to gear up for the job," says Dr. Frank Booth, a University of Missouri professor who specializes in exercise adaptation (particularly the ways in which the body is impacted by exercise or lack thereof). "If you exercise a couple of hours before or after the meal, it won't do as much for you." In case you want to cheat while you still have an afterburn going, belly up to a buffet that is high in carbohydrates. "Right after exercising, your stores of carbohydrates are used up. The muscles really suck out the carbs." Therefore, they will quickly process a fresh load.

Best Time to Lay Low

Obviously, it's when you've dabbled in insider trading or swindled millions from your sickly dowager of a grand-mother. But there's also another, less clear-cut time: when you're out of a gig and need to generate new work for yourself. Forget that this is exactly when you'd seemingly want to be in people's faces and on their minds.

This contrarian answer is posited by Norm Macdonald, a TV actor who's had more than his share of ups and downs (star of *Saturday Night Live,* fired from *Saturday Night Live* after NBC boss Don Ohlmeyer deemed him unfunny; star of eponymous TV show, said show canceled after a couple of seasons; star of second show, which was canceled as well). He remembers the advice he was given between gigs: "My managers and agents always told me, to keep going on talk shows and doing interviews. They told me that I couldn't be invisible."

Norm disagrees. His belief is that it's better to devote your time and energy to devising something new and to let the public—whoever your public might be—see you only when you have something truly cool and unique to show them. "My approach has always been to tell every-body that I've been kicked out of show business because nobody wants me. Then I come back when I've got some-thing to talk about. I hate to see guys appearing on Leno's or Conan's show, being asked what's happening, and all they can truthfully say is, '*This.*'"

Best Time for a Punctual Flight Departure

Common wisdom holds that you want to book as early a departure as possible, before broken-down planes and congested runways conspire to wreak havoc with flight schedules. David Learmount, operations editor at the airline industry trade publication *Flight International*, explains that, statistically, an airline's first takeoff of the day is often delayed because lots of carriers are trying to get passengers into the sky simultaneously. "You want to schedule to leave after that first wave and before the second wave," says Learmount. "And the deeper into to the first wave you get, the more likely you are to encounter problems."

Learmount suggests checking with your local airport or airline and figuring out when the various waves take place (they're different for every airport). Usually, there are lag periods between them, when flight schedules catch up, and thus planes are more likely to take off punctually. He points out that late-night departures are frequently on time, but there is a caveat: "At the end of the day, if an aircraft has gone unserviced till the evening, it will come in late, and that might be the aircraft they put you on." Therefore, your takeoff will be delayed.

It is also worth noting that more flight cancellations happen in the middle of the day than in the morning, when freshly repaired planes minimize the likelihood of mechanical failures. "As the hours wear on," says

Learmount, "airports experience the domino effect—and if you get caught in it, it can crush your travel plans."

Best Time to Go to the Emergency Room

If you can schedule the slicing open of a finger, or the breaking of a toe, or a decisive knockout blow to your noggin, do it between eight A.M. and noon on a Wednesday, Thursday, or Friday. According to Dr. Robert McNamara, past president of the American Academy of Emergency Medicine and current chairperson of the Temple University Hospital emergency department, the busiest days in an ER are Monday and Tuesday. "People have the weekend off and don't feel so well, but they don't bother dealing with it until the beginning of the work-week—when they should be rolling into their offices," says McNamara. "Plus, there are a lot of doctor's appointments scheduled for Monday and Tuesday, and a person who appears to have a complex situation will often get sent to the emergency department. On top of all that, fewer beds are available in the ER on those days because more surgeries take place [at the beginning of the week, rather than in the middle or at the end]."

The busiest times in emergency rooms are noon to midnight, though holidays (including—*surprise*—New Year's Eve) are slow, as people aim to avoid hospitals on celebratory days. In July, the emergency rooms usually experience an influx of inexperienced residents. Speed over to the ER on nights, weekends, and during summer months and you will most likely encounter substitutes for full-time ER doctors.

In terms of seasons, the least busy time in an emergency room is spring. Trauma injuries don't really rev up until the summer, and, says McNamara, "there are not a whole lot of illnesses going around. Wait till winter, though, and that's when the respiratory infections kick in."

☻ *Emergency? What Emergency?* ☻

Thelma Gundlach felt her arms go numb and her vision turn fuzzy. She sensed a stroke coming on and had a friend rush her to the emergency room at a hospital near her home in Modesto, California. Gundlach, sixty-nine, expected to be seen right away. Instead, she waited four hours in an emergency room jammed with other patients. Gundlach survived (her stroke was a minor one), but she now says, "It's unnerving to think about going back there."

Lots of other patients feel exactly the same way. A 2000 study conducted by the National Center for Health Statistics revealed that patients with nonurgent problems (where life or limb are not at risk) wait an average of sixty-eight minutes to be seen, up seventeen minutes from 1997. "Generally, if you come in with a chest pain, you'll get seen quickly," says Robert McNamara. "Otherwise, you'll wait hours—as many as twelve, based on what I've witnessed."

While it's no fun thinking about getting hurt, McNamara suggests you do some planning ahead for an injury or illness. For instance, scout around your neighborhood for an emergency room with a fast-track area that will address minor complaints quickly. "Also, if your emergency is not life-or-death," he says, "take a few minutes to call and find the hospital with the shortest wait."

Best Time to Buy Fish

Most fish stores get deliveries on Monday and Thursday, for the week and weekend, according to Mitchell Slavin, manager of New York's M. Slavin & Sons, the biggest fish distributor in the tristate area. "The safest time to buy fresh fish is Tuesday or Friday," Slavin says, explaining that the extra day gives the retailer time to get the new stuff out for sale. "To ensure that what you buy is fresh, the fish should feel firm and have good eye appeal. If it doesn't look appetizing, walk away."

Best Time to Sweat a Perp
(or, for Anyone Who's Never Seen *NYPD Blue*, Question a Crime Suspect)

Right after the crime's been committed—but not before you have enough evidence with which to hang the guy.

"You don't want to give the suspect time to come up with an alibi or destroy evidence," says George Brejack, captain of detectives with the Passaic County Prosecutor's Office in Paterson, New Jersey.

Brejack, once known as "the psychic cop" and lauded for his ability to wangle confessions in the course of solving seemingly unsolvable crimes, adds, "But you also have to make sure that you've got enough information to question him with. That's at least as important as getting him into your office right away. Otherwise, he realizes you don't have anything on him, he'll think you're a jerkoff, he won't be scared, and he won't agree to cooperate in order to try saving his own skin. The other thing is that you need to schedule it in your space, at a time when it's convenient for you and, preferably, inconvenient for him; it adds an extra degree of anxiety and reduces the likelihood of the guy being able to think on his feet."

Recalling a particularly bad character, someone suspected of sexually abusing and killing a young girl, who was found with strangely patterned scratches on her body, Brejack says he let the perp stew. It gave him and his investigators enough time to discover that the springs below the guy's mattress perfectly matched that scratchy pattern pressed into the girl's torso. "It proved that he stashed her under the bed after the murder," Brejack says. "Once he realized that we knew this, it scared the hell out of him and made it easy for us to get the guy convicted. Remember, once somebody knows you're fishing"—rather than being in possession of damn-

ing information, no matter how scattered it might be—
"you're screwed."

Best Time to Thank Your Parents

Smiling broadly, Mary Marcdante suggests, "Right now." Author of *My Mother, My Friend: The Ten Most Important Things to Talk About with Your Mother*, Marcdante adds, "There are no times soon enough to tell our parents how grateful we are for their raising us."

She acknowledges, however, that she recently used the event of her own birthday to send her folks a thank-you note. "I told my parents that I am glad to be alive and I thanked them for the gift of life. I pointed out a few details—like the fact that my father used to take me to skip stones—and they helped my parents to recall some great memories. It's the sort of thing that rejuvenates you and them."

Best Time to Get Comped at a Casino

Before you arrive. In gambling lingo, the word *comp* means "a freebie"—a free room, free meals, free drinks, free airfare. To get all of those things, you need to be a big gambler, one who's wagering thousands of dollars on each bet. But to get *some* of those things, you can be a guppy, as opposed to a whale—as long as you know when to time your request for comps.

Steve Cyr, subject of the book *Whale Hunt in the Desert* and king of the casino hosts (that is, the guys who bring in players and divvy up free stuff) at Las Vegas's Golden Nugget, says that you should get all the comps agreed to as soon as you make hotel and air reservations. "Otherwise, if you wait until you're in town," he says, "the host will tell you to keep playing and that he'll see what he can do for you before you leave. But by that point, you no longer have any leverage. He'll give you what he wants to give you, and you won't have a choice but to take it. If you speak with him ahead of time, and get a line of credit or wire five thousand or ten thousand dollars or whatever into an account, then you can convince him to guarantee a certain number of comps. Among the easiest for him to offer are room comps and free limo pickup from the airport."

And if he doesn't? "Tell him you'll take your business elsewhere. If he's a good host, he will take a shot with you. It's a gamble—you might not spend as much time playing as he would like or wager as much as he expects you to—but this business is all about taking risks"—regardless of which side of the felt you're on.

⊛ *See How They Comp* ⊛

Max Rubin, author of *Comp City: A Guide to Free Gambling Vacations,* has literally written the book on how to offset losses with freebies—and he knows the formula that casinos use to justify them: "Take what they perceive to be your average bet, multiply it by 40 percent, and the casino will give you that back for every hour of play." Let's say you average one hundred dollars per hand of black-jack and that you play for four hours per day over a four-day vacation. You can then expect to get $640 worth of comps.

Asked how to get the best returns for your time at the gaming tables, Rubin has a few suggestions:

- Sit at a crowded table where the play is slow (the casino clocks the time you spend at the table, not the actual number of hands you play; the fewer hands you play per hour, the less you are mathematically certain to lose).
- Make your biggest bets when the pit boss is watching (he's the one who reports how much you're betting, and if he sees you making a few large bets, he'll assume you're doing it with relative consistency).
- Always go for the soft comps (these are from enterprises owned by the casino, as opposed to outside vendors; casinos tend to be much more generous when they're giving you dinner at cost rather than having to pay full-freight for platters of sushi at Nobu).

By the way, if you think that Rubin's strategies suck the juice out of gambling, he'll be the first to agree: "This isn't about making money by playing at the tables. It's about having fun and getting free stuff."

Best Time to Pose Nude for *Playboy*

If you haven't done it between the ages of eighteen and twenty-five, your chances of getting inside the mag that once featured a naked Marilyn Monroe are slimmer than a Playmate's baby toe. "That is the typical age range," says Gary Cole, photography director at *Playboy*. "But it depends on the woman, how well she takes care of herself"—smoking and drinking don't help—"what kinds of genes she has. We did a whole spread on women over forty, and we have occasionally photographed women over fifty. Vicky LaMotta [wife of boxer Jake LaMotta, on whose life *Raging Bull* was based] was over fifty when we shot her—though she was extremely attractive and the exception."

Cole acknowledges, however, that there are other factors in his age game as well. "From a straight visual perspective, eighteen is best—this is all biological, like the Discovery Channel—though you sometimes see an eighteen-year-old who has not yet physically matured," he says. "She may have baby fat, and six years later she'll be more attractive because she's slimmed down, or is doing her hair differently, or has developed a degree of savviness that suddenly comes through when she's in front of the camera. We've had girls come to the studio, do a Playmate test, get rejected, then come back several years later and be accepted. A woman who appears one way in person can look very different when viewed through a lens. Sometimes it makes her skin appear worse. Or else it exposes a great side of her personality that never comes through in face-to-face meetings."

Playboy shoots most of its nude images outdoors, and Cole avoids doing them in the middle of the day. Never mind that it increases the possibility of a pedestrian stumbling upon the set, he's more concerned about the light. "It can be harsh and glaring during the midday hours," says Cole. "So we try to do outdoor shooting early in the morning or late in the afternoon." He hesitates for a beat, then adds, "Of course, though, the best models are good at any time of the day."

Best Time to Travel to the Caribbean

"Late October through early November is when price and weather converge," says Paul Niskanen, owner of Cruise Masters travel agency in Portland, Washington. "The hurricane season is over, it's getting dry, and you still benefit from low fall fares. The other time with good value and good weather is early December, when a lot of people like to stay home and fuss with the holidays."

Best Time to Rattle an Interview Subject

When he's about to give you a canned response. Bill O'Reilly, host of *The O'Reilly Factor,* on Fox News Channel, prides himself on pressuring people to admit the truth. He faced a particular challenge when confronting George W. Bush prior to the 2000 election. "He walked in, and I could tell that Bush had all kinds of rehearsed answers," says O'Reilly. "So I hit him with a real haymaker right at the beginning: 'Governor, you said that Jesus was your model as a personal philosopher, and that's pretty good'—he liked that; you could see his face perking up. But then I added, 'That being said, what would Jesus think of you executing all those people in Texas?' He had no prepared response, had to think of something to say, and, in the process, forgot all of his rehearsed answers."

Best Time to Buy Fruit

Unlike vegetables—which are sweetest when their seasons start—a piece of fruit generally peaks from the middle to the end of its growing term. "The earliest fruits of the season lack flavor," says David Karp, the acclaimed "fruit detective," who consults with the country's top gourmet shops and is in the process of writing a book on "fruit connoisseurship." "During the early part of the season, the fruit-development period is short. Fruits go from bloom to bud to maturity so quickly that they don't develop the desired sugars and aromatics. Plus, there is a financial premium for early-season fruit, and that's when growers are most likely to rush their products to market in order to enjoy extra profits."

☀ *Judging a Fruit by Its Skin* ☀

By the time you bite into a perfect-*looking* peach, it is too late to do anything about the mealy pulp beneath the skin. That's why you want to examine the goods before you pay for them. Karp offers a few pointers for increasing the odds that the fruit you buy will be as delicious to the tongue as it is to the eye.

Oranges: They should not be puffy and soft, but they should not be rock-hard, either. Don't be turned off if there are greenish streaks; that could simply mean that the skin hasn't been dyed (as is often the custom with oranges).

Green grapes: When they begin to get a golden cast, grapes are perfectly ripe and great for eating.

Plums: They should feel spongy and be aromatic.

Peaches: If they're rock-hard, they're not ripe. If they're too soft, they will probably get bruised in your grocery bag. Focus on the peaches that have sweet, pronounced smells.

Apples: They should be hard on the outside and have a little bit of an aroma—but don't expect this to be as obvious as the peach's scent.

Bing cherries: Plump and dark are the preferable characteristics.

Dates: Harvested in August and September, they are stored and sold throughout the year. The dates you buy in late summer and early fall should be soft, plump, and delicious. By late spring, they've been sitting around for nearly twelve months and tend to granulate, while the skin becomes tough and wrinkly.

Best Time to Go into Business with a Spouse

When you've reached the professional and personal point where you can operate like true work partners, without marital feelings getting in the way. This means you can be tough and objective and argue intensely—but keep it from affecting dinner at home with the kids. "I've seen it work very well for couples who can separate their business lives from their personal lives," says Marjorie Brody, career expert and etiquette columnist for BusinessWeek Online. "One person needs to be able to acquiesce to the other and split workplace roles, without ever allowing it to become an ego thing."

Beyond chemistry and emotional maturity, a husband and wife both need to provide something concrete for the business. "They must bring a skill set to the table that the other person doesn't have," says Brody. "And it's got to be something that will help build the company." Asked if she'd ever consider entering into a joint venture with her husband, a dentist, Brody answers in a half-kidding tone: "It would not work. I keep telling him how to run his business, but he never listens to me."

Best Time for a Comfortable Mammogram

This is based purely on breast sensitivity. In light of that, Silas Deane, spokesperson for the National Foundation for Cancer Research, says the prime time for a mammogram is "the week after a woman has started her menstrual cycle. For most women, the best time of day is late morning or early afternoon, when breasts tend to be least sensitive."

Best Time to Get Your Car Repaired

According to Ray "Clack" Magliozzi, cohost of National Public Radio's *Car Talk* and co-owner of the Good News Garage in Boston, the best times of year are spring and fall. "In the spring, you want to get your car into shape so you can drive it all summer—the season when you tend to go farthest from home. A disastrous breakdown will be expensive and might ruin your vacation," says Magliozzi. "In the fall, you want to make sure your car battery and charging system, belts and hoses, and antifreeze protection are all in good shape."

Asked if early January, after the Christmas holidays, is a good time to find eager mechanics in need of cash, Magliozzi says that it makes sense on paper but could backfire in reality. "Because they need money, mechanics might try selling you stuff you don't want and look for problems that aren't there."

Finally, Magliozzi says, the best time of day to take your car in is the early morning. "Most shops get their parts ordered and their days organized in the morning." So by getting there early, you increase the likelihood that your car will be looked at immediately, parts will be in hand by lunchtime, and repairs can be completed later that afternoon. "Go in at two P.M., instead of nine A.M., and you'll lose a whole day."

Best Time to Get Serious About Wine

You're sitting in a four-star restaurant, enjoying a delicious meal. Suddenly, you find your taste buds placing less emphasis on the steak au poivre and more on the sublime cabernet sauvignon with which you're washing it down. According to Peter Morrell, owner of the highly touted wine retailer Morrell & Company in New York City, this is the moment when you've crossed over and become serious about cabs and chards and all the other great grapes. "Maybe," he says, "you're suddenly dipping your nose in and appreciating the bouquet as much as the taste. That's when you reach the point where you cannot enjoy a meal without a glass of good wine—and you find it very difficult to drink anything bad. The positive news, though, is that wine making has improved to the point where there are a lot of well-made inexpensive wines."

But, as the man who once sold a double magnum of

Château Margaux 1900 for $29,900, Morrell acknowledges that money doesn't hurt. And after you make a bundle of it can be the best time to get serious about wine at a whole different level. "Some people put money into cars and planes," he says. "Others put their money into building and stocking wine cellars. That's when you make the conscious decision to embrace wine as a lifestyle as well as a beverage. It's like finding religion."

☺ *Wine Cheat Sheet* ☺

Owning one of the top wine shops in New York City, Peter Morrell can drink rare vintages every night. But he doesn't. "Typically," he says, "I drink wines that sell for ten to twenty dollars per bottle. And they're terrific wines." How does he do it? "The key is to find good wines from less popular regions. What drives the price of wine is demand. Find these lesser-known wines and you will drink better for less money. In some cases, you can have four good wines for the price of one expensive wine. I'll take that every time." Here are five of Morrell's favorite moderately priced offerings and the pricier wines they can stand in for.

- **Château Laussac** is merlot-based and sells for $29.95. It mimics St. Emilion, *premier grand cru classé,* which sells for fifty to sixty dollars a bottle. It is best matched with lamb.
- **Dallas Conte** is a Chilean cabernet sauvignon.

Bottles from the 2001 vintage sell for $9.95. It mimics a twenty- to thirty-dollar cabernct sauvignon from Northern California. Serve it with steak.

- An Australian shiraz called **Woop Woop** retails for $11.95. It tastes like a thirty-dollar shiraz from France. Drink it with stews and grilled ribs.
- The **2001 Jekel** is a chardonnay from Monterey County, California. It sells for $10.95 but would be worth twice that if only it came from a little farther north—in, say, Napa Valley. It is best with all kinds of fish and chicken.
- A sweet-tasting **Monbazillac** from France will sell for $16.50 and might be mistaken for a late-harvest wine from the Sauternes region, which would set you back a good fifty dollars. Uncork it when you're serving foie gras.

Best Time to Sleep Late

Saturday morning. Most people choose to sleep in on Sunday and use Saturday as the day for getting an early start on running errands. According to Kirsty Kerin, consultant with Circadian Technologies, a Boston-based company that researches sleep and productivity, you will feel a lot better if you choose Saturday as your day of rest. "It is human nature to sleep roughly one hour later than you did the day before," she says. "Biological clocks want to run twenty-five hours per day. So if you sleep an extra hour on Sunday, then you are going up against a two-hour differential on Monday morning. That's what accounts for the Monday-morning blues." Kerin suggests catching up with sleep on Saturday and rising at your normal weekday time on Sunday.

Whatever the day, teenagers are notorious pressers of the snooze button, and the parental instinct is to drag them out of bed, insisting that they shouldn't doze through a beautiful day. Kerin believes that this is wrongheaded. "Teenagers usually have owl-like behavior. They stay up late at night, then need to rise ridiculously early in order to make it to school on time. So when they're sleeping in on weekends, they are simply making up for sleep deprivation during the course of the week. Let them sleep," she says, even if that does mean a rough morning on Monday. "They need the rest."

Best Time to Fire Someone

Midweek, at the end of the day. "That way, there's no perception from others on the workforce that this was done after getting a week's worth of labor out of someone," says Susan Schoenfeld, senior managing editor of *Business and Legal Reports,* which publishes compliance papers for major corporations. Pointing out that an online poll done by *Business and Legal Reports* shows that 40 percent of those surveyed believe that Friday is the best day, Schoenfeld attributes this to executives waiting till they close out their payrolls and attempting to provide a weekend-long bridge between the day an employee gets canned and the morning when everyone else returns to work.

But sometimes it's less than prudent to pick a specific day. "Most importantly," adds Schoenfeld, "you should fire an employee as soon as your realize that the person has done something wrong"—that is, has committed the unpardonable sin that warrants a dismissal. "If it happens midweek and you wait till the end of the week, the employee may continue with the behavior that caused his problems in the first place. And if he senses he's going to be fired, he can bad-mouth you to clients, damage property, steal files, or copy a door key. Get the person out as soon as possible."

Best Time to Be Photographed

"Not early in the morning—which is what a lot of people think," says Timothy Greenfield-Sanders, who photographs for *Vanity Fair* and has shot portraits of the biggest names in pop music, art, and business. "You've been sleeping on one side of your face or the other. So it's puffy. You want to start with hair and makeup at ten-thirty or eleven and get on the set by noon. That's what you'd do if you were Paris Hilton or Babe Paley. By the way, you don't want to be photographed late in the afternoon, either—when you're tired and it shows on your face and in your eyes."

While he's on the subject, Greenfield-Sanders provides a tip about how to tell if the person shooting you isn't as seasoned as you might hope: "There's definitely a best side for everyone. It's an aesthetic interpretation. I can tell instantly, just by looking at a person, which way he or she should face. If the photographer can't tell you your best side, there's a good chance that he doesn't know what he's doing."

Best Time to Purge and Organize

While it's obviously ideal to be continually diligent—tossing out papers, giving away old books and clothing, relegating a half-working computer to the trash—few of us can do that on a regular basis. Barry Izsak, president of National Association of Professional Organizers, feels our pain. He suggests that, under relatively normal conditions, the opportune time to reorganize is before moving or painting. "Why deal with schlepping all your old stuff and having to put it away?" he asks, sounding perfectly reasonable.

Under more dire circumstances, he says, "The best time is when you run out of storage space or can't find anything and are becoming dangerously unproductive. People develop irrational physical attachments to their things. Sometimes somebody suffers a loss and hangs on to stuff from the past as a way of compensating. But, at a certain point, the lightbulb goes on and you realize that you need to lose the clutter."

☺ *Five Steps to a Newer, Neater You* ☺

Before you can be serious about getting organized and tossing out junk, you need a game plan. When Barry Izsak and employees of his company, Arranging It All, go to work for a client, they initiate a five-point strategy. If they're working on a kitchen, here's how they map it out.

1. Break the job into small, manageable pieces so that you can complete one section of it at a time. Otherwise you'll be overwhelmed. First spend an hour organizing your Tupperware drawer. Then move on to the pots and pans. Rather than looking at it as a whole day spent organizing a kitchen, view it in hour-long increments. And remember this rule: If you haven't used something in the last year, it goes out the door.

2. Clear the space that you're going to organize and start to sort, while purging what you don't need. When putting stuff back, remember to keep like things together. If you have a junk drawer, put the paper clips in one area and the pencils in another.

3. Purchase the proper storage devices, such as dividers and add-a-shelves, so that you can create distinct areas devoted to specific things. For spices, get turntables. For cabinets that are too deep, get rolling pullouts. A lot of kitchens have

big lazy Susans in the corners of cabinets. The key to organization is to make retrieval easy.

4. Replace the items and store them closest to the point of use. Put stove-oriented utensils in a drawer near the stove. Have glasses and plates in a cabinet near the dishwasher. Situate all things where they can be reached most efficiently.

5. Monitor the system and always put things back where they belong. If you don't, the whole operation will break down—and you'll have to go through this all over again.

Best Time to Serve Jury Duty

There are two kinds of people who serve jury duty: those who want to get on trials and those who do not. If you fall into the latter category, try to serve during the summer or around Christmas or Thanksgiving. "Judges and lawyers take days off during those times of year," says G. Thomas Munsterman, director of the Center for Jury Studies at the National Center for State Courts in Washington, D.C. "Also keep in mind that at the end of the week, there are fewer new jury panels to be drawn into; for the sake of continuity, few trials start on Friday. So if the trial you're being considered for fails to happen, there won't be another jury for you to be moved to."

If, by some chance, you do want to serve on a jury, Munsterman suggests this: "Mondays and Tuesdays are the busiest days of the week for new trials. And the first week of January is typically very heavy, due to the layoff of the Christmas holidays. Early fall gets busier as well, but it's not quite as pronounced as in January."

Best Time to Start a Diet

Though there is no calendar date that is best suited for starting a diet—losing weight for the holidays is fine, but with that time-oriented mind-set, it'll be tough to stay slim for the coming summer—there are internal signals that tell you the time is right. "You want to reach the psychological point where nothing will get in the way of losing weight," says Dr. Vincent Pera, medical and program director for the Miriam Hospital Weight Management Program in Providence, Rhode Island. "The best indicator is that you have made up your mind to elevate your diet to a very high level in your life." To abet that, Pera says, you want to start a diet when your day-to-day dealings are stable. "Job loss and disruptive family situations will make it difficult to stay focused on losing weight."

Best Time to Run into a Burning Building

When the smoke smells acrid. According to Dennis Smith, former fireman and author of the classic firehouse tome *Report from Engine Co. 82,* acrid smoke is usually the bitter by-product of burning food—rather than an indication of a burning building. "The scent of burning wood, on the other hand, means that the fire probably started inside the walls, it's most likely electrical, and now the building itself is on fire," says Smith. "But even with food, the heat buildup can be very high and it can explode quickly."

A secondary response is that if you are a civilian, there is no best time to run into a burning building. But if you're a fireman, it's always the best time. Or, as Smith tersely puts it, "If the walls aren't cracked and people aren't yelling on the fire escape, the job requires entry. Firefighters don't ask whether or not it's the best time."

However, they do recognize the worst time: "When you pull up to a factory or tenement and see flames pouring out of the windows. This tells you that the fire has grown in such intensity that it was able to break through the glass. That's when you call for assistance and know you're going to be there for a while."

Best Time to Start a Road Trip

"About six in the morning," suggests Ken Smith, a co-author of *Roadside America* and a serious enough driver that he put 250,000 miles on his automobile's odometer while researching the book. "At that hour, your system is alert, there's not much traffic, and you can put two hundred miles under your belt before breakfast. Then you sit down in a diner and enjoy your pancakes while everyone else is stuck in traffic."

☺ *Four Sites Every American Should Visit* ☺

If you're going to hit the open road, you might as well learn something in the process. Bill O'Reilly, host of *The O'Reilly Factor,* an immensely popular show on the Fox News Channel, is a hard-core history buff who has traveled throughout the United States. Here's where he'd send you for a firsthand education.

Gettysburg: "This country's most important battle took place there, and the caretakers haven't changed a blade of grass on the battlefield. You see exactly where the soldiers fought and get a sense of how many were killed."

Lexington and Concord: "They're located outside of Boston, and a trip there will teach you about the minutemen and how the Revolutionary War began."

Mount Rushmore: "It's an amazing achievement, and the Black Hills are a great setting. After seeing Rushmore, you go down to the nearby towns and find out about Wild Bill."

Pearl Harbor: "It's important for Americans to see where we were attacked. A visit there brings the whole thing back to life."

Best Time to Fess Up

When you have information on a bigger fish who can be fried. "Usually, though, the biggest fish do best because they come in first—on their own," says Ian Comisky, a Philadelphia-based tax litigator whose clients have included the notorious IRS cheat Leona Helmsley. "Look at Andrew Fastow, from Enron. He pleaded guilty and got a ten-year sentence, but he's going to testify against the guy above him. And at the same time, he got a much smaller sentence than the guy below him. Had Fastow waited, that lower guy might have come forward and Fastow would have been worth a lot less."

The other good time, according to Comisky, is simply when you can't sleep at night, because you're so racked with guilt or fear, and somebody is dangling a way out. "If the feds come knocking at your door and offer you some kind of a deal"—he's being literal here, but you can take *feds* figuratively, in case you're not an out-and-out embezzler or tax dodger—"you can assume that the train is getting ready to leave. If you want to take it, you'd better move quickly."

Best Time to Do Damage Control

Maybe you've chosen not to fess up. There were no bigger fish to turn in. Or you just didn't have it in you.

But still, you've been caught red-handed, dead-to-rights, whatever. In that instance, you should have seen the potential nightmare coming and should have begun executing a damage-control plan before it became a necessity. Jonathan Bernstein, president of the Los Angeles–based public-relations firm Bernstein Crisis Management, has learned that most crises—personal and professional—can be prevented by making a few minor changes in how you operate.

When the minor, or major, changes have not been implemented, then it's time for plan B. Let's say you get caught cheating on your spouse—the marital equivalent of embezzling millions. Bernstein suggests that you do the very thing Martha Stewart neglected to do after lying to the SEC: Act humble, admit you did something wrong, and apologize. "Then you promise to do your very best to make amends," he says. "It goes a long way toward establishing damage control. And it can result in a reconciliation with your audience—in this case, your wife—though other times things may have gone too far to be mended."

What creates the irreparable situation, the one in which you have little choice but to lie low and try to keep the damage from being completely devastating? When you're a repeat offender in the mode of compulsive gambler Pete Rose. "The humble thing only works once or twice," warns Bernstein. "At a certain point, you have to change." Or else.

Best Time to Make an Outsize Charitable Donation

Looking to contribute a new wing to your neighborhood hospital? Or a study center to your alma mater? Do it when you have lots of money and no kids. So goes the advice of Jamie Oliver, the London-based bestselling cookbook author and chef. In 2002, he bankrolled a London restaurant called 15, staffed it with fifteen underprivileged kids who'd never before set foot in a professional kitchen, and turned the whole thing over to a trust, out of which he can't pull a dime. The setup is that Oliver, who's made many millions from his cookbooks, would create a situation where kids can learn on the job and he would make no money from it.

It sounded like a good idea at the time, back when his wife seemed unable to have children. But then, just after he committed to the project, she became pregnant. Good bloke that he is, Oliver didn't back out. But he does acknowledge, "As soon as you have children, you become slightly more selfish and slightly more inward-looking. You want to build a nest and have a comfort zone. And you also want to stash away your extra quid."

Putting your money into a nonprofit restaurant is no way to do it. And while Oliver admits he would never have undertaken 15 if he knew kids were in the offing, he points out, "I've gotten at least as much out of the experience as the students have."

Best Time to Buy Caviar

If you like caviar, there is no markedly bad time to buy it or eat it. However, according to Mark Russ Federman, owner of Russ & Daughters, one of New York City's top retailers of caviar, there is a prime time—particularly if you're going for top-end fish eggs from the Caspian Sea: "Spring and fall," says Federman. "Those are the two times of year when caviar gets brought in." More specifically, fresh catches of Beluga, Sevruga, and Osetra make their collective way to retailers during the months of October and May. "That's when," says Federman, "the eggs are perfect; they're not mushy. The taste is clean; it is not tinny or overly salty. The caviar has a clean, fresh sea taste."

If you plan on buying Caspian Sea caviar, keep in mind that the stuff from Russia is almost always frozen—which is fine, although not ideal in October and May. Due to fishing regulations, very little is coming out of formerly Soviet waters these days. So, if it's Russian, it has probably been in cold storage for the last few years. Federman opts instead to sell, and eat, fresh (or at least fresh*er*) Iranian caviar. "And," he says, "I find Osetra to be consistently the very best in terms of texture and flavor."

Best Time to Bowl a Perfect Game

In the early evening, just before bowling leagues take over the alleys. According to Jason Couch, a professional bowler with seventy-six perfect games to his credit and more than one million dollars in PBA winnings, bowling lanes are rigged for leagues. "Late in the afternoon, prior to league nights, lanes are oiled from the ten board on the right to the ten board on the left, which results in there being an excess of oil in the middle," says Couch. "That makes for more forgiving lanes and increases your odds that the ball will stay in the center." It definitely lays the groundwork for higher-scoring games, which will keep league players coming back.

The worst time to bowl a perfect game is just before or just after a PBA tournament. "For members of the Professional Bowlers Association," says Couch, "the wax is evenly spread across the lanes. So we don't catch any breaks. It might be the reason why I have fifty perfect games as an amateur and only twenty-six as a professional."

There's another thing that will reduce the likelihood of your nailing twelve strikes in a row: "For those who bowl once a week, the best time to replace your ball is annually. Otherwise, you get dead-ball syndrome. It stops hooking and won't curve through the pins the way you need it to."

⊕ *Jason Couch's Five Foolproof Steps* *to Throwing Strikes* ⊕

1. Take a deep breath and concentrate on what you need to do before stepping up to the approach.

2. Set yourself in line with where you want to throw the ball. You want your ball to roll over the second arrow, right along the oil line.

3. Get your muscles nice and relaxed. Normally, you'd want to be four or five steps back from the foul line. In your second step (for a five-step bowler), you begin the process of pulling the ball back. You push it away from your body and let gravity bring it down. You don't want to use any force. You want to be as fluid as possible.

4. For the backswing and follow-through, keep your arm straight, as if it were a swinging pendulum. Then you release the ball with your thumb coming out first and the fingers second. That gives the ball a spin, which allows it to roll through the pins more forcefully and have some hook.

5. Stand there and track the ball as it barrels down the lane on its way to the pocket's sweet spot. Then go into a semicrouch and watch the pins scatter. Make a fist, crook your elbow, jerk back your arm, and say, "*Yessss!*"

Best Time to Drop a Dime on Someone

Henry Hill, on whom Ray Liotta's character in *GoodFellas* is based, never wanted to leave the Mafia or squeal on his fellow mobsters. But he knew the ideal moment in which to turn state's evidence—or, in the parlance of the street, *drop a dime*—before his options became increasingly limited. "The best time to talk to the feds," says Hill, "is a split second before the boys are gonna whack you."

He insists that it was literally a life-or-death situation. "They called my wife, told her to come down the street to speak with them about something, and that's when I knew that they were going to kill us both. There was a point in my life when I would have sooner put a gun in my mouth than become an informer, but I was terrified for my wife and myself. I had no choice."

How did it feel to turn on the guys who had once been like brothers to him? "Everyone I helped put away was a homicidal murderer with no conscience," says Hill, whose recent memoir is entitled *Gangsters and Goodfellas*. "So I tried to justify it that way. But still, it took me a long time to realize that I had done okay. After eight years of feeling like a piece of dirt, I've gotten my soul back, and that's the best reward."

Best Time to Go to the Doctor

First thing in the morning. "We schedule four patients between eight o'clock and nine, three of the four will be here within the first hour, and the plan is that those three will be out before nine A.M.," says Dr. Howard Glazer, president of Physicians Who Care, a patient-advocacy organization made up of doctors.

The Madison Heights, Michigan–based family practitioner says that the other efficient time for a doctor's appointment is right after lunch—"It's when we come back with a clean slate again"—and he warns that if you develop a history of being a no-show, it might not matter what time you schedule your appointment for. "When a patient develops a reputation for coming late or not coming at all, doctors double-book their time slots."

Best Time to Deal with the IRS

Immediately. This may sound like obvious advice, but, according to the experiences of Richard Yancey, former revenue officer for the IRS and author of the memoir *Confessions of a Tax Collector*, at least 50 percent of delinquent taxpayers ignore notices from the agency. "The IRS will not forget about you," warns Yancey, adding that it has a ten-year time period in which to collect money. "The absolute worst time for somebody to have gotten a visit from me was when they had one year left on the time limit. The IRS is loath to lose an assessment, and, with so little time remaining, I left no stone unturned in trying to collect the money."

Yancey insists that there are two good reasons for not attempting a ten-year dodge. "For starters, once they catch up to you," he says, "you will be billed enormous amounts of interest—twice as much as what the bank charges—for every day that you don't pay the taxes you owe; I've seen people wind up owing more in interest than they owed in taxes. And once you make an agent drive to your house and chase you down, he's not going to be as friendly as he would have been if you'd gone to him and attempted to work out a deal." And things can get even worse, says Yancey: "If you're not home, the agent will knock on your neighbor's door and ask when you usually get home; the agent will go to your office, to your kid's school. It will get embarrassing and will no longer be between you and the IRS."

Is there an upside to all of this? Yes, says Yancey: "You only have a 1.03 percent chance of getting audited in the first place."

Best Time to Buy Your Kid His First Set of Golf Clubs

When he celebrates his tenth birthday. According to Eddie Merrins, the pro at Bel-Air Country Club in Los Angeles, and former coach of the UCLA golf team (seven of his college players are currently on the PGA tour), that's the age when "they're old enough to listen to instruction and make sense of what you tell them. As far as getting into the game and understanding the mental approach, ten years old seems to be the age of reason."

Merrins, a golf fanatic himself, points out that there's nothing wrong with letting your kid swing a club as soon as he's strong enough to lift it. And it's a good idea to begin teaching early lessons by example: "Take the boy or girl to the driving range and let them watch you hit golf balls."

As for the best time of day for teaching kids to golf, Merrins suggests morning till early afternoon. "They seem to be most alert during those hours," he says, adding that golf should always be presented as a fun pastime, with no hint of the frustration that taints the sport for many adults. "It's about playing games and having a good time. Or else the kids won't do it. I make them swing at targets for rewards. If they hit a certain object out on the fairway, they receive a free ball. All kids have competitive instincts, and this is a way to whet those instincts."

⊕ *How to Find a Golf Instructor Who's Better Than You Are* ⊕

Finding a reliable golf teacher can leave you deeply in the rough. "Too often a guy with a good shtick will get your money," says Wayne DeFrancesco, golf instructor at Woodholme Country Club in Baltimore and one of *Golf* magazine's one hundred best teachers in the United States.

Maybe that explains why the average male golfer's handicap has stayed around sixteen for the past ten years—even though there are now twenty-seven thousand PGA-certified golf pros in the United States (five thousand more than in 1997). With golfers spending upward of two hundred dollars an hour on coaching, why isn't the overall game getting better? "Bad teaching," says DeFrancesco. He contends that too many coaches aren't even decent golfers. You should hire an instructor who has earned a Class A designation from the PGA. That means he's spent around two and a half years training to be a pro and taken thirty-six hours of continuing education every three years. (To check, call the PGA at 561-624-8400.) Also, ask the pro for his scores in recent tournament play. As DeFrancesco puts it, "If you're a good teacher, you should be able to teach yourself to shoot in the seventies."

Best Time to Raise Capital

Adeo Ressi knows how to make other people give him money—and it has nothing to do with a *Sopranos*-inspired shakedown. Since the mid-1990s, he's managed to fund several high-technology companies with more than twenty-million dollars from venture capitalists (people who find new businesses in which to invest their clients' millions). He says it's best to anticipate closing your deal between mid-March and mid-May. "The first quarter of the year generally gets taken up with other stuff—limited-partnership reporting, taxes, things like that," says Ressi, adding that entrepreneurs sometimes get lucky at the end of the year, when they approach the money people just as they need to fill their investment quotas—but nobody with a burgeoning business should rely too heavily on luck. "It's so competitive to get funding that you want to hit the venture capitalists when they have their money and are looking for something to do with it. You definitely want to close before summer begins, when everybody's away and fewer deals get done." One other piece of advice from Ressi: "Start the process of getting your VC money in December. It will take four months before you're on anyone's radar."

Best Time to Buy Jewelry

Back when Elvis was King and his second home was a sprawling suite at the Las Vegas Hilton, Mordechai the Jeweler was the man he'd phone up for everything from diamond pendants for recent conquests to fresh TCB rings for new members of his posse (augmented by a lightning bolt, the rings' initials stood for "taking care of business," and were originally cast by Mordechai). Over the years, Mordechai endured three A.M. wake-up calls from Presley (once, Presley required half a dozen women's rings—immediately), handled ungodly requests from Mike Tyson (including a pair of diamond-dripping wristwatches that went for four hundred thousand dollars each—to be paid for at a later date), and created ultraglitzy pieces that would impress a sultan (boxer Floyd Mayweather purchased a custom-made diamond-encrusted fist-size medallion, shaped like the horse insignia on his favorite Ferrari).

For all those folks, the best time to buy jewelry was the exact moment when they wanted it. And they paid for the privilege (even Tyson eventually coughed up the money, following a bit of legal wrangling). Mordechai suggests that the rest of us should time our exquisite purchases for the months when things slow down in the jewelry biz: "July and August; there are no gift-giving holidays and people tend to focus more on taking vacations and less on buying diamonds," says the man who now owns a Vegas-based chain of stores called, appropriately enough, the Jeweler, though he still does lots of custom work for high rollers and the like. "You can bargain better when there is less business. And, to an extent, that's also true in January [after the holidays] and April [after tax season]. Stores need cash flow and their owners are willing to negotiate."

Best Time to See the Northern Lights

The northern lights rank high among the world's most stunningly beautiful natural wonders. Despite the fact that you may be in precisely the right place—close to the sixty-fifth geomagnetic latitude, or, more simply, Dawson City,

Canada, in the northwestern part of the country—if it happens to be precisely the wrong time of year, you run the risk of missing an unforgettable storm of rainbow-hued illumination in the otherwise pitch-black sky.

According to Dr. Charles Deehr, professor emeritus and auroral forecaster at the University of Alaska's Geophysical Institute in Fairbanks (another good locale for viewing), prime time is during the two weeks of the new moon in March. "You don't want the moon competing with the lights," he says. "And you want to go during the spring equinox"—as opposed to the fall equinox, in September—"because you have a better likelihood of the sky being clear. There is a 30 percent chance of bad weather in the spring and a 60 percent chance in September."

What can one expect to see in the Canadian heavens on an optimal night in March? "A huge display of light. The whole sky becomes filled with luminous colors, and the overall impact is indescribable." So, really, you have to go witness it for yourself this coming spring.

Best Time to Retain Information

Depends on your age. Lynn Hasher, professor of psychology at the University of Toronto, headed up a study that shows how different people hold on to information at different hours, due to "attention regulation"—that is, the times reserved by the brain for absorbing what you read and hear. "For college students," she says, "the best time to retain information is between four and five in the afternoon. Due to changes in circadian rhythms, adults over the age of sixty are more likely to remember what they learn early in the morning."

☕ *Memory Triggers* ☕

Matt Graham is a top-level Scrabble player, the kind of guy who can lay down a seven-letter word while snagging points by building on three other words along the way. Memory serves as his primary tool, and he is obsessed with keeping thousands of obscure Scrabble words—such as *xi, picolinate,* and *fremd*—percolating in his brain. Between games at the invitational World Scrabble Championship, Graham offered a few pointers for remembering and recalling obscure words at a moment's notice.

Read and remember: He reads words into a tape recorder, then plays the tape while he is sleeping.

Vicks trip: While committing certain words to memory, Graham dabs a bit of Vicks VapoRub under his nose. Then, during a match, when he can't find a word he needs, he rubs the Vicks across the top of his upper lip. Graham says that the scent triggers words he studied while smelling the rub.

Yeast feast: Brewer's yeast is high in RNA, which, Graham says, is good for fine-tuning the brain. He chugs a liquid form of the stuff from a metallic shaker and uses it to wash down capsules of memory-enhancing smart drugs.

Fugue you: Before a big match, or while studying words, Graham slips on headphones, plugs into a Walkman, and listens to Bach's fugues. They supposedly stimulate the brain.

Best Time to Replace Your Home's Roof and Windows

You don't want to do either of these jobs on extremely warm days, because they both fall into the category of *hard work*—whether you're doing it or someone else is—and spiking temperatures make the job that much more painful. "But it can't be too cold, either," says DIY handyman Jeff Wilson. "A lot of weather-sealing products that you employ for windows can't be used when the temperature dips below fifty degrees. At that point, the stuff won't set up quickly enough and it'll become sticky." Not to mention the drawbacks of enduring even a modestly chilly day without your roof or windows. So schedule the job to be done sometime in the spring or early fall.

You also need to make sure that there'll be at least eight hours of dry weather immediately after the windows are installed. Wilson learned this lesson the hard way: "Things got wet right after I put in a window. Rain poured down the side of the house, the caulk hadn't had a chance to dry, and it stained the exterior of the building."

Obviously you want dry, temperate weather when you're working on a roof. Less obvious is that you want to lay down the roof in the morning (humidity levels rise as sundown approaches) and paint it in midafternoon. "If you let paint dry in direct sunlight, it dries too quickly and leaves streaks."

Best Time to Clean Up a Murder Scene

After police have devoted the better part of a year to investigating the murder and have left the crime scene sealed with black-and-yellow tape. "That way," says Ed Evans, owner of Biosafe, an Orange County, California, company that specializes in cleaning up messy deaths, "the human element has decomposed. Flies and maggots have done their work. Rodents have had their feeding frenzy. And by the time I show up, it's just a lot of dust and mites that need to be swept away."

Evans concedes, however, that those in his line of work are rarely so lucky. Usually, the body is fresh and the room is a mess. In those instances, sooner is better than later—especially if the victim was shot in bed. "Blood leaches through the sheets to the mattress, to the carpet down below, and into the wood," Evans explains. "So you have to go in and take out everything—from the blood-soaked mattress to the subfloor. Then there're the skull fragments. Skull fragments can scatter around and cause a real problem. They're sharp as razors and really cut you up badly if you unexpectedly stumble upon them."

When it comes to days of the week for the job, Evans prefers Sunday, when he can listen to gospel music on the radio and enjoy a weird kind of peacefulness that permeates the scene. Best of all, family members of the deceased tend to be in short supply. "I don't like to clean when they're around," says Evans. "Everybody is stressed and talking. A lady will tell me not to cut her husband's favorite T-shirt as I try to get it off his body. And whatever you do just seems to take longer."

On the upside, though, relatives on the scene can keep what they want from the murder site and save Evans from needing to figure out whether or not to dispose of, say, a blood-spotted bag of golf clubs. "We'll put aside anything for the family—except electrical appliances. When you turn them on, any blood that might have gotten inside will start cooking. That can be pretty gross. It's one smell that still makes me gag."

Best Time to Buy New Technology

Everybody wants to have the newest, coolest handheld devices and chip-driven gizmos. But it's incredibly uncool when your pocket-size jukebox plays the Velvet Underground after you've programmed it for an afternoon of the Velvet Fog. The key to avoiding such glitches is to buy the gear soon enough for it to be cutting-edge, but not so soon that it's got more bugs than one of Ed Evans's cadavers. Peter Rojas, founding editor of gizmodo.com and current editor of engadget.com, Web sites devoted to all things technological and awesome, advises that the best time to buy new technology is three months after the item's release.

He says it's the happy medium between cool and cold. "If you wait six months, it won't be cool anymore—but you will get a good price because the next wave of technology is right around the corner," says Rojas. "However, if you wait even two weeks after the first release, you will see *some* improvements, because all the early adopters will be calling in problems to the manufacturer." Within three months, he explains, your device should be completely exterminated.

Rojas counts himself among those early adopters, and he has his share of war stories: a wireless card that slowed down his laptop's MP3 player (he ditched the card), a first-generation multimedia PC "that was superbuggy," and a digital video recorder that hooked directly into the cable line but failed to record requested shows. Was that last one from personal experience? "No," says Rojas. "I have TiVo and don't even have cable. If I want to see something, I find it on the Net and download it onto my hard drive. Then I take it with me and watch it wherever and whenever I want."

Best Time to Reveal a Potentially Disturbing Fetish to Your Lover

After you've had sex together three times. This surprisingly exact strategy comes from sexual-advice columnist

Dan Savage, and it actually makes sense. "By this point, you've shown the other person that you are capable of having regular sex and enjoying it," he says. "They know that you're not a guy who needs to be wearing, say, women's high heels in order to get off. Tell the other person before you have sex that you're into cross-dressing, and he or she is liable to think that you need to wear nylons and panties all the time."

How you break the news is almost as important as when you break it. "Having a fetish is not like having leukemia," dryly states Savage, whose weekly alternative-newspaper column is called "Savage Love." "You want to make the other person see that it's a fun twist, rather than a horrible impediment. Then, once you've established yourself as a somewhat kinky person, the other person should feel free to share some fantasies with you. You've suddenly given your partner license to be as kinky as possible."

And that can be a lot of fun for both of you.

Best Time for a Massage

Depends on what you want the massage to accomplish. If the massage is designed to reduce the aches and pains that keep you awake at night, have it prior to bedtime. Sports massages should be administered just before and just after your workout. And if you've been in a car accident, or sustained a traumatic injury, and want to get relief from lingering pain, it won't matter when you get the massage, as long as you have a few minutes to relax after it's over.

All of this comes courtesy of Linnea Hemphill, a Denver-based massage therapist who worked on a study with the University of Colorado and the Denver VA Hospital to investigate the impact of massage upon the comfort level of cancer patients. It reduced nausea and anxiety in the test subjects, and, explains Hemphill, it can benefit the rest of us, as well. "A ten- or fifteen-minute chair massage before, say, a business meeting is a good thing," she says. "It will improve your alertness. This was proven through a study conducted by the Touch Research Institute at the University of Miami Medical School. Students there were given math problems to solve before and after their massages. They did better after." The EEG results revealed heightened patterns of alertness in their brains, as well.

⏰ *Massage Cheat Sheet* ⏰

Before you let someone start pounding your sore muscles, make sure you know what to ask for. Diana Turk, massage supervisor at the venerable Golden Door spa in Escondido, California, offers some insights on what to expect when the rubbing begins.

Swedish massage: Activates the circulatory system and increases joint mobility. Also serves to trigger activity in the lymphatic system, which promotes relaxation. Characterized by long, gentle strokes and kneading.

Deep-tissue massage: Isolates and works on specific muscles, tendons, and ligaments. More intense than a Swedish massage; best suited for injury rehabilitation and relief of back pain.

Shiatsu massage: Focusing on pressure points, it's an acupressure massage that is very targeted, without a whole lot of kneading or stroking. Good for dealing with specific maladies that are not necessarily muscle-related—such as headaches and menstrual cramps.

Watsu: Massage takes place in shoulder-deep water. You spend most of the massage floating, as the therapist works your body and holds you up. It's not a very hard massage and is more about nurturing than it is about relaxing specific muscles. It's the sort of massage you want to have right before vegging out or taking a nap.

Thai massage: One of the few massages that you get with your clothes on, it goes from the tip of your toes to the top of your head. No kneading or stroking, but lots of intense pressure placed on specific points. Designed to balance the inner workings of your body and leave you with an overall feeling of well-being.

Best Time to Downsize

Sarah Susanka, author of *The Not So Big House* and *Home by Design,* is an architect who also happens to be a proponent of scaling back on possessions, on the size of your house, on the enormity of your bills. She believes that people can live happier lives with fewer—but better—things. In her mind, it's always the right time to downsize. For the rest of us, though, this minimalist's minimalist keeps it short and sweet: "It's when you realize that all your stuff is ruining your life."

She's being a bit dramatic here, but the point is the old cliché about *things* not making us happy. "There comes a point when you realize that having possessions will not satisfy the hole inside you that needs to be filled and nurtured," she says. "Reflexively, people build bigger houses for themselves when they make more money. Why not use that money, instead, to make your existing house work in a way that's perfect for you? Or take six months off from your job and do something that you've always been dying to do. Having a big house with rooms you don't really need makes you feel uncomfortable in your own home. To have a room waiting to be filled, but which never gets filled, creates a bad feeling."

If you do have such a room, and you're perfectly happy with where you live, Susanka offers a radical notion: "Make the room useful. Maybe it's a big room, where you can do jumping jacks every morning. Or maybe it's a small room that can be turned into a great little studio. People think about personalizing a space as bringing things inside it. I think it's more about reshaping the space—lowering ceilings, curving walls, improving the light—to make you feel better about yourself and where you live."

Best Time to Rent a Car

After you take a cab—or, even better, a free shuttle bus—from the airport to your hotel. Beyond the hassles of dealing with rental-car agencies in crowded airports, you're actually paying dearly for the privilege of going from the plane to a shuttle bus and then to a car. "Renting from the airport is brutal," says Amy Ziff, editor at large for travelocity.com and author of the site's "Travel Tips from A to Z" section.

On top of the premium that might be charged for an airport rental, she says, the taxes can be astronomical: "In Houston, the airport rental taxes are 71 percent of your total. New York City has the highest rental prices in the country." If you must rent a car at an airport when coming into the Big Apple, she advises that you can save considerable money by flying into nearby Newark International and renting a car there instead of at JFK or La Guardia.

The other important time-related issue is that you should reserve your rental car as far ahead of time as possible. Since the rental companies do not require credit cards to secure cars, you might as well get in early and snag any discounts or deals. And if you need to cancel? Who cares. "There are sometimes free upgrades and special rates for those who book a few weeks ahead," says Ziff. "What you should never do is let the agent up-sell you—that is, get you to upgrade your car when you are at the rental counter."

Finally, keep in mind that most rental companies get their fresh fleets of cars in September and October (Florida outlets tend to get new models in November and December). That's when one rental agency might be flooded with a certain type of premium automobile—say, an SUV or a convertible—and, under those conditions, at that time, Ziff says, "You can sometimes get more car at a lower price."

Best Time to Throw a Knockout Punch

According to Thomas "Hitman" Hearns, the great Detroit-based cruiserweight who successfully unloaded the decisive blow on forty-six hapless professional opponents, "There's only one best time: When you've got him groggy. That is when you need to take your shot. And you do it by delivering your best punch at that exact moment."

Just one problem, though. Your best punch is probably the one that made him groggy in the first place. So don't you want to knock him out with something he's not expecting? "Yeah," says Hearns, whose most lethal blow was a left hook. "That's why I'd hit the guy with a couple of left hooks, get him groggy, and then start throwing other punches. After a while, I'd forget about the left hook and let him forget about it, too. Then, just as he's thinking about other stuff, and figuring that I won't use the left hook again, that's when I throw the knockout."

After pausing a moment to let all of this sink in, Hearns offers a final piece of advice: "But it's more than the punch. Legwork's involved as well. You put all your weight behind the shot, gracefully step into your opponent, then just let him have it." And if you're Thomas "Hitman" Hearns, you watch with satisfaction as another palooka hits the canvas.

Best Time for Surgery

Common wisdom had long held that the best time to go under the knife is first thing in the morning. That way, the thinking went, your skin-slicing doctor will be fresh. Not so, according to a study conducted by Janet Starkes, professor and chair of the kinesiology department at McMaster University in Hamilton, Ontario. "Surgical techniques are not that different from other motor tasks," she says, adding that motor tasks include shooting baskets and pitching baseballs. "And when it comes to performing motor tasks, your first one of the day will not be as good as the ones that immediately follow. It's why sports teams warm up before games." In other words, the best time for surgery is midmorning, after the doctor already has an operation or two up on the scoreboard.

Another study hints that more complications arise from surgeries done at night. Maybe it's because the physicians are tired from operating all day. Starkes suggests that the late-night curse can be mitigated when the surgeon doing the cutting is seasoned at the procedure in question. "If you get someone who is very skilled at a task, then the task feels less complicated and won't be as taxing," she says. So the doctor will be able to perform more surgeries and make fewer mistakes.

☺ *The Unkindest Cuts* ☺

Did you hear the one about the Florida woman who was admitted to a hospital with a brain hemorrhage? The surgeon operated on the wrong side of her brain. Or how about the Brooklyn hospital where an ophthalmologist mistakenly operated on a patient's good eye?

These OR blunders would be laughable if they weren't so awful. Euphemistically referred to as "wrong-site surgery," such mishaps rose from sixteen nationwide in 1998 to fifty-eight in 2001 to seventy in 2003. To protect yourself from becoming a victim of a directionless doctor, your first defense is avoiding incompetent hospitals.

The Joint Commission on Accreditation of Healthcare Organizations does qualitative studies on health-care facilities across the country and posts the results on its Web site, www.jcaho.org. Second, don't cut your surgeon too much slack. Before you go under anesthesia, discuss with him exactly where—and why—he wants to make incisions. Don't let him break skin unless you're completely satisfied with his answers.

Best Time to Have a Safe Flight

Early on a summer morning, several days after a severe air accident, according to David Learmount, operations editor at the airline industry trade publication *Flight International*.

Not surprisingly, the fewest accidents happen during daylight. So that means you want to take off when it's light, but you need to check what time you need to take off in order to ensure a daylight landing, as well. It's also safest to fly in the summer. But if you must fly in the winter, keep in mind that more accidents happen on takeoff than on landing. So you'll help your less-than-optimal odds for safety by leaving on a winter morning and, if need be, landing after dark, rather than the other way around.

The reason for enhanced danger in the winter has nothing to do with 747s skidding down icy runways. "If the temperature is at or near freezing, including just above it, you can get ice on the airframe and the wings will stop working," says Learmount.

As for flying in the wake of a serious accident, Learmount explains that it's the time when airline employees tend to be most conscientious and most conservative in how they assess situations. "When Swissair Flight 111 crashed into the sea off of Halifax back in 1998, the problem was caused by an electrical fire," says Learmount, pointing out that the tragedy could have been avoided if the pilot had been willing to inconvenience his passengers by making an emergency landing. "Right after that Swissair crash, if there was even a hint of an electrical fire—and there were a few similar incidents that followed—they landed the plane at the nearest possible airport and got the passengers off. Previously, aircrews would have just kept going. On Flight 111, they didn't want to piss off passengers with a delay. So they didn't do that. But instead, they wound up crashing the plane."

Best Time to Put Money into a Retirement Account

Smart investors are counterintuitive, and the ideal time for socking away retirement money is when everyone else is selling.

That's why James Cramer, former hedge-fund manager and current cohost of *Kudlow & Cramer* on CNBC, feeds his retirement accounts in September and October. "September is the cruelest month [for Wall Street]; October has been the scene of many a crash and minicrash," says Cramer. "So why not commit to putting equal amounts of money each month into your IRA or 401(k)? We Cramers wait for extreme [downturn] days to put the money to work. Is it foolproof? No. But these months have seen the lows for many years now, and we get the best prices when they throw the sales."

Best Time to Get Your Name in the Newspaper

Any weekday. "Getting a client into the paper is not just for the sake of having his name mentioned," says publicist Bobby Zarem, a larger-than-life character who was influential in launching the careers of Sylvester Stallone, John Travolta, and Dustin Hoffman. "It's a way of announcing this client's accomplishment to the other media. You want people of influence at *Time* and *Newsweek* and the television networks to read it"—the idea being that they might then be inclined to run their own stories. "But there is a tendency on the weekends for people not to look at newspapers as carefully as they do during the week."

However, Zarem is quick to point out that sometimes it makes sense to shoot for a weekend placement: Weekdays are more competitive, while, generally speaking, weekend columns and features (Saturday through Monday) get cranked out by Friday afternoon. The compressed schedule leaves reporters hungry for material and more likely to run with less-than-juicy tidbits, which would be shunned during the week. "It all comes down to how newsworthy your item happens to be."

Best Time to Get a Complimentary Room Upgrade at a Hotel

When you arrive late and the place is packed. The logic here is that hotel managers are generally not keen on giving upgrades for no reason, but they have to give them if all the standard rooms are filled. And since hotels typically overbook, to account for cancellations, the manager will have no choice but to bump you up.

However, Jack Naderkhani, general manager of the Beverly Hills celebrity haunt Raffles L'Ermitage, says there are other factors that might make one time particularly prime for a room upgrade. "We give the upgrade to someone staying for a single night," says Naderkhani. "If someone is going to be with us for five nights, we would rather not put that person in a suite." He explains that this is because it might then be awkward to downgrade the guest to a regular room. "If we see that we're full, we will upgrade a one-nighter, even if he arrives in the morning—as long as we don't expect any other one-nighters to be checking in later that day. And we also remember the loyalty of our guests. We will be quicker to reward a guest who stays here constantly. He'll check in and think that we're such nice people. But he doesn't know that we have to upgrade *somebody*."

What about using the timing of a birthday, an anniversary celebration, or a trip with your wife and kids to get in a hotelier's good graces for an upgrade? Naderkhani, a gentleman who prefers to give people the benefit of the doubt, has heard it all before. Maybe that's why he suggests that an honest reason and an advance request can win the day. "Just make it clear that you realize you're asking for a favor, you don't do it on a regular basis, and you won't do it again anytime soon."

Best Time to Nail a Tough Restaurant Reservation

Japanese restaurant Nobu is a notoriously challenging place when you're trying to snag a rezzie. The Manhattan eatery books thirty days ahead, and weekend dinners sell out within ninety minutes. While it's a hassle to commit to a restaurant reservation so far in advance, the bigger problem is getting through on the telephone. Nobu's reservations line is often busy for entire mornings. "That's why the best day for making a reservation is Saturday or Sunday," says Dana Sardinha, Nobu's reservations manager. "It's easiest to get through then because secretaries and assistants are off from work. So they're not sitting at their desks and continually speed-dialing our number for their bosses."

But there are alternative best times. Let's say you want to have dinner on a Tuesday night. Chances are there will be cancellations (all those people who booked a month ahead couldn't envision what would be happening thirty days in the future), but, says Sardinha, if you call on Tuesday, there will already be a long wait list. "It's better to phone us on Monday," she explains. "You might be able to get a confirmed reservation right then and there. Or, at the very least, you should get a good spot on Tuesday's wait list."

What if you're super-spontaneous and you just want to pop in for dinner with no advance notice? Choose a weeknight and arrive early. "If you get here at five-forty-five, when we start serving dinner, you stand a good chance of being seated," Sardinha says. Nobody is waiting at that hour, and restaurants always have last-minute no-shows.

⏱ *Culinary Magic: Turning a Side Order into a Cash Cow* ⏱

Dine at a high-end steak house and you can expect to pay a lot for your sirloin. But it's the extras that will carve you up. Just ask a fellow we'll call Mr. L. He and his wife shelled out $63.90 for two steaks at a Gallagher's restaurant near their home—but that was just the beginning. "What gets me," he says, "is the baked potato. They charge just under five dollars for a one-dollar potato." Bryan Reidy, a Gallagher's spokesman, says, "It's a sixteen-ounce potato, and that price is normal for steak houses."

Gallagher's is hardly alone in getting a lot extra for its extras. French fries at Ruth's Chris go for up to $5.95; a romaine and iceberg lettuce salad at Morton's is $6.95. Jim DeJoy, purchasing manager for the Culinary Institute of America at Greystone, in St. Helena, California, contends that some restaurants turn their vegetables into cash cows. For instance, he says four pounds of lettuce that should produce twenty portions will cost a restaurant eight dollars—or forty cents a serving. However, he has seen some dining spots charge $6.50 per salad—roughly, a 1,500 percent markup.

Best Time to Ask for a Raise, Other Than When You've Gotten a Better Offer Elsewhere

The timing for this one has nothing to do with the economy or your company's finances, says Stephen M. Pollan, lawyer, financial consultant, and author of *Second Acts,* which focuses on how to accomplish goals during the last half of your life. Nor, he adds, should you time a raise request to your wife's pregnancy or a mortgage increase. "Those things are immaterial," says Pollan. "The best time to ask for a raise is when you can prove you are entitled to one. The way you find out if you are entitled to it is by speaking with other employers and peers in your industry. Armed with that, you go back to your employer, express gratitude for the professional growth he's afforded you, and show what the market pays for people like you. Then you ask him to reconsider your compensation. It's unassailable."

Pollan also suggest a few time-related considerations: "Don't do it near the end of the fiscal year. You'll be creating new overhead just as everyone is trying to bring in moderate numbers. Don't ever do it on a Monday. At the beginning of the week, people are busy making up for what they didn't do on Friday. And don't do it on Friday, because your supervisor will be only half there. Too close before lunch is no good, either. Very early in the morning is a good time. After lunch is good, because a body that's full of food is a more docile body. You want to get the person when he is in a lull and can concentrate exclusively on you."

Best Time for a Comeback

Before you're completely out of the game. At least that's the way Eddie Kerkhofs, owner of Le Dome, once Hollywood's hot celebrity restaurant, sees it.

He's basing this opinion on more than just his own experience. Back in the day, the places to be on Sunset Strip were Le Dome and Chasen's. Through the 1980s and into the 1990s, though, the aging clientele of Chasen's disappeared (that is, died off or decided to go to bed early without having a nightcap of Chasen's famous chili), while Young Hollywood found trendier places in which to dine and deal.

In 1995, Chasen's went out of business and then, two years later, backed by new owners, attempted a comeback—with spectacularly unsuccessful results. In late 2002, before twenty-five-year-old Le Dome was forced to face the same awful fate as its former competitor, owner Eddie Kerkhofs took a drastic step: "I brought in three partners, we closed for a year, and we did a total renovation. The place was looking old, and we needed to attract younger customers if we wanted to remain in operation."

In November 2003, he launched his comeback with a new chef, a new look, a cool waitstaff, and a younger clientele, which gets off on eating within earshot of kitschy icons like Jackie Collins. Insisting that in its new incarnation his restaurant is doing just fine and will be around for another twenty-five years, Kerkhofs acknowledges that properly timing his comeback probably saved his skin: "Once you're out of business, nobody really wants to know about you anymore. You lose your space, your staff, your customer base. By recognizing the problem, and doing something about it before it becomes critical, you save yourself a lot of aggravation."

Best Time to Do Magic

"When nobody's anticipating it," says David Blaine, who cut his teeth by performing card tricks in the streets of New York but is now most famous for undertaking tests of endurance, which include living in a block of ice and being buried alive. "Even if you're dressed up as a magician and the audience is anticipating something, magic that's unexpected is always the strongest."

For Blaine, much of this lies in the presentation, context, and timing—like when he approached a woman who was standing at a bus stop in London, struck up a conversation, and began complaining about the girl who had dumped him. The idea being expressed here was that she broke his heart badly enough to cause a physical reaction. Blaine began pressing his fingers against his chest, pushing, pulling, and kneading, until he appeared to prod beyond the skin and extracted what looked like a bleeding, beating heart. "The timing for that was effective," says Blaine. "It was the last thing that she expected to see."

Timewise, there's also a lot to be said for, as Blaine puts it, "doing the magic when you feel like doing it, rather than when someone asks you to. You do it when you can create the moment. Magician and author Henning Nelms wrote that no matter how astounding a trick may be, it suffers if it has no point. If I can make a sandwich appear in your pocket, so what? But, if you told me you were hungry, and I waited till then to make a sandwich suddenly appear in your pocket, then it has a point. It seems real and amazing and has a true-life narrative, rather than just existing as a magic trick."

Best Time to Catch Fish

Never mind those guys who rise at dawn and sleepwalk to their docks and dinghies. "Last hour of sunlight, when the fish are feeding, is absolute prime time," says Dave Precht, editor in chief of *Bassmaster* magazine. "Sun penetration is low, so that keeps it dark under the water and reduces the possibility of the fish realizing that they are snapping at a lure rather than at food. Plus, they won't be able to see you wading in or floating in a boat. Finally, the water warms up throughout the day, making the fish more active and raising their metabolism."

Being that Precht is something of a bass specialist—though he'll fish for anything that swims—it's worth getting the skinny on the best time of year to catch his fish of choice. He says it's the end of winter or early spring, with March being the best month for people in the Southeast (head north and wait till April, when the water heats up; in Florida, Texas, and Southern California, go after your bass in January and February). After lying low and not eating much during the coldest months, says Precht, "bass are hungry when springtime temperatures kick in and they're in a rush to fatten up for spawning."

Asked how concrete his predictions are, Precht fires back, "We keep records of all this. The ten-pounders"—about as big as a freshwater bass will get—"are almost always caught between January and April. And it usually happens in the southern states, where bass tend to be bigger because they have longer seasons for growth."

☕ Best Time to Catch the Rest ☕

Maybe you don't like freshwater bass. No problem. Precht lays out a schedule for catching five other popular swimmers.

Trout: Best time is when the temperatures are dipping down, as trout are adapted to cool, fast-running water, below fifty-five degrees and just above freezing. They range in size from less than ten ounces for brook trout to up to six pounds for rainbow.

Bluegill: Best time is throughout the summer, in water that is seventy degrees or warmer. They are very active in shallow water and would rather eat bugs than fish—hence, summer being the peak season. They respond best to live bait—worms and crickets—and are small (from twelve ounces to one pound) but strong. Bluegills travel in schools and make for good eating if you can catch a bunch of them.

Crappie: Best time is in the spring, when water temperatures hover between fifty and sixty degrees. They eat minnows and are easiest to catch with those on the hook. Crappies can be found across the United States and tend to congregate in underwater drop-offs. They range in size from one to three pounds.

Striped bass: Best time to catch this oceanic cousin of the freshwater bass is between September and October, when they tend to run close to shorelines up and down the East Coast. You attract them using jigs, which resemble saltwater minnows. Striped bass weigh from five to twenty pounds and are best reeled in after you've worn them out a little bit.

Best Time to Buy Your Neighbor's House

"When he doesn't think you want it," says Ralph Roberts, author of *Walk Like a Giant, Sell Like a Madman* and quite possibly the most successful real estate broker in America (he claims to close on more than six hundred properties per year). "If he thinks you want it, he'll think it's worth more to you than it is to a person who's just buying that single piece of property."

And he's probably right. That's why, if it does get offered to you at a halfway reasonable price, according to Roberts, you ought to jump on it without a whole lot of niggling, which could sour the deal. How much of a premium you should put on a piece of property that will make your life markedly better is impossible to calculate, though Roberts, who's a notorious haggler, points out that the opportunity may literally be once in a lifetime.

This is something he knows about firsthand. "I wanted to buy a property from the guy next door," he recalls. "I was going to split this land with the neighbor who lived two houses away. But then that neighbor backed out, I hesitated, someone else bought it, and I lost the property forever. Now I'd pay anything for that piece of land. It would have dramatically improved my lifestyle."

Best Time to Work Late

On Tuesday nights, between six and nine, the hours when human productivity peaks. "The biological clock has an alertness profile, between six and seven in the morning, to help you wake up," says Kirsty Kerin, who specializes in advising corporations on how to maximize nocturnal workforces. "Then, between four and five P.M., the alertness profile rises again. It starts to peak at six. Ending your workday at that hour is counterproductive—in terms of work, though it does mean that you will be driving home when you are most alert." And, presumably, that reduces the risk of auto accidents during evening rush hour.

The reason you want to select Tuesday as your late night has to do with when you are best suited to be tired in the morning—and assume that you will be if you work till nine or ten the night before. "First and second days back at work"—that is, typically, all day Monday and Tuesday morning—"are not especially productive because you are out of your routine," says Kerin. "If you are sleep-deprived on either of those days, forget it, they'll be shot." There's another practical reason for working late on Tuesday: If you need to spend a second night in the office that week, you can do it on Thursday and have a good rest between the two sessions of overtime.

Best Time to Take a Home Pregnancy Test

One week after you think your period should have arrived. "The egg in a woman's body may be fertilized, but it can be nine days before a hormone called HCG—which is what the home pregnancy test detects—is produced," says Allen Wilcox, senior investigator with National Institute of Environmental Health Sciences. He conducted a study that showed 10 percent of pregnant women received false negatives after they took the pregnancy test around the day they expected their period to arrive. "Even though some women have their period like clockwork, they do not have their ovulation like clockwork."

So they may not know, with 100 percent certainty, when the ovulation is in relation to their period. "The problem is that if you think you're not pregnant, you may find yourself doing things you shouldn't"—smoking and drinking, for starters; dropping ecstasy and boxing, for finishers—"when there is a baby forming inside you. Within a week, there is a very low percentage of having a false-negative reading. But if you have money to burn, and just can't wait to find out, you can do the test every day for a week and feel comfortable with the ultimate result."

Best Time to Raise Your Bet

You're sitting at a blackjack table in Las Vegas and, if you're like the typical player, you're betting based on hunches and streaks, raising wagers when you're winning, reducing them after a string of losses. Professional blackjack player Rick Blaine says that the only time to make a huge bet is when you know that the first card you'll be dealt is going to be an ace.

How might you ascertain this? Maybe it's because the dealer accidentally flashed the card before sliding it your way. Or maybe it's because she's your roommate's best friend and has signaled you that this is the case. Never mind that such an act is considered collusion and can land both of you in a holding cell for the night—or worse—if you know that the next card is an ace, Blaine says, you have a 50 percent advantage over the house and you ought to bet big.

The other, more likely scenario is that you've seen lots of twos through sixes come out during previous hands. "Let's say half the deck is dealt and that out of the twenty-six cards dealt, there were six extra-low cards," says Blaine, author of *Blackjack in the Zone*. "You've got about a 12 percent advantage. Let's say you're making an average bet of twenty-five dollars. The appropriate bet would be about three hundred dollars. And this is conservative. There's no guarantee you'll win, but if you give up your advantage, you're playing at a disadvantage."

⊕ *Guide to Basic Strategy* ⊕

You may never learn to count cards like Rick Blaine, but if you plan on playing any blackjack at all, you ought to play the game right. Basic strategy, which was developed, along with card counting, by an MIT professor named Edward O. Thorpe, is the perfect way to play blackjack. It reduces the house edge to less than 0.5 percent and gives you a fighting chance if you can exercise decent money-management skills (quitting after winning or losing no more than a set amount). Here's how it works:

1. Stick on all hard totals of 17 or higher.
2. When the dealer shows an up card of 7 through ace, keep hitting until your cards total 17 or more.
3. Stick on hard totals of 13 through 16 when the dealer shows an up card of 2 through 6.

4. Stick on a hard total of 12 against the dealer's up card of 4 through 6.

5. Double down on all hard totals of 11 against every one of the dealer's up cards except an ace.

6. Double down on all hard totals of 10 against every one of the dealer's up cards except an ace or 10.

7. Double down on all hard totals of 9 against the dealer's up card of 3 through 6.

8. Always split aces; always split 8's.

9. Never split 10's; never split 5's.

10. Split 4's against the dealer's up card of 5 or 6.

11. Split 6's against the dealer's up card of 2 through 6.

12. Split 9's against the dealer's up card of 2, 3, 4, 5, 6, 8, or 9—but not 7.

13. Double down on hands of ace/2 or ace/3 against the dealer's up card of 5 or 6.

14. Double down on hands of ace/4 or ace/5 against a dealer's up card of 4, 5, or 6.

15. Double down on hands of ace/6 or ace/7 against the dealer's up card of 5 or 6.

Follow these moves with robotic consistency and it's guaranteed you'll do better than the guy sitting next to you, who is probably making random decisions, without a bit of science behind him.

Best Time to Visit Europe

For France and all of Central Europe, October is the dovetailing time of year for decent temperatures and dipping prices. "The weather is still holding up, all the French kids are back in school, and the American tourists are gone," says Howard Lewis, owner of Chartwell Travel in Los Angeles, one of America's top travel agents for European vacations. "November is a little bit colder, but you get all the great winter dishes and lots of wonderful mushrooms. Then, if you get too cold, you can go down to Italy, where it is a little bit warmer." The surprisingly good time for visiting Paris specifically, says Lewis, is August. "Most of the Parisians are gone and you get all kinds of deals there that month."

In terms of England, Lewis says, "If you're willing to put up with some bad weather, but want low prices, go there in May, October, or November. That's when the locals pay more attention to you and are all-around friendlier because there are so few tourists. You'll feel like you have the whole country to yourself."

Best Time to Play Basketball

Skip your morning game of hoops (or tennis, for that matter) and save it for the late afternoon or early evening. According to Dr. Cedric Bryant, chief exercise physiologist for the nonprofit American Council on Exercise, "For sports that require dexterity and reaction time, it's best to play between noon and nine P.M. This was determined through studies in which individuals' performances were measured in tests of reaction time. The other factor, though, is core body temperature. It tends to be highest between four and six P.M., so that might be the ultimate peak time. Researchers believe that the elevated temperature speeds up the conduction of nerve impulses and enzymatic activity, which combine to make chemical reactions happen quicker at the cellular level of the body." In other words, if you're going to try dunking, five P.M. is go time, baby.

Best Time to Plead the Fifth

Bruce Cutler is well known as the chrome-domed pit-bull attorney who spent many years helping famed Mafia kingpin John Gotti earn the nickname "the Teflon Don." In the course of keeping charges from sticking to Gotti, Cutler wielded the Fifth Amendment—which allows a person to avoid testifying in court if what he is going to say may incriminate him—as routinely as Gotti's henchmen wielded revolvers. "I would say that *all the time* is the best time to plead the Fifth Amendment, particularly when you're dealing with the authorities," says Cutler. "The exception would be if you have decided to work with them." Of course, though, if you've hired somebody like Bruce Cutler to represent you, chances are good that you will not be turning state's evidence anytime soon.

Considering this for a beat, Cutler adds, "There are moments when a person feels that what he says will get him out of a jam, but that is rarely the case. Even if you believe you are justified in doing what you did—let's say you shot somebody in self-defense—you need to remember that you are dealing with law enforcers, who may not feel the same way about these matters as you do. That's why I advise just about all of my clients to plead the Fifth."

Best Time to Launch a Paradigm-Shifting Business

After everyone has written off your chosen sector for dead. Such was the situation for Nick Denton, a technology entrepreneur whose advertiser-supported Web site, gawker.com, is all the rage among New York City's media cognoscenti. The site, which provides cheeky commentary, along with links to pop-culture reports and media gossip on the Net, revels in petty celebrity feuds and big shots getting their comeuppance. Think of it as a self-deprecating *Spy* magazine for the Internet age.

Denton launched gawker.com in 2002; had he done it a few years earlier, when the Internet was roaring, he could have easily gotten lost in the high-tech sauce—and would probably be out of business right now. "The timing made it easy for me to grab attention," he admits. "When we launched, people were pathetically grateful for anything interesting to read on the Web."

Plus, the bursting of the new-economy bubble made it easy for Denton to find out-of-work talent on the cheap, and a good deal of his required technology had already been developed—at great expense to others. Though Denton talks about having limited ambitions when he started the thing up, he's certainly not holding back right now: His company's already launched a sex version of gawker (fleshbot.com), a D.C. version of gawker (wonkette.com), and an L.A. version of gawker (defamer.com).

After making the whole operation sound like a lark, he expresses his ambition of seeing gawker grow to a hundred times its current size, while crowing about being able to walk a sharper edge than more overtly commercial sites. "It's hard for an established media property to launch a site like mine and maintain [the irreverent] tone," says Denton. "They tend to have concerns that go beyond amusing the audience. At gawker, we don't care about insulting people, and the editor doesn't worry about not being invited to parties or being unable to social-climb."

❂ *Nick Denton's Favorite Blogs* ❂

Blogs, or Web logs, are essentially personal Web pages where individuals rant, rave, and loudly share their views. As gawker partially focuses on finding the most compelling blogs on the Net—and linking to them—it only makes sense that Denton would have something to say about his favorites. Here are six of them:

kottke.org: media-centric musings; similar to gawker, but with a spikier edge and totally noncommercial.

Electrolite: left-wing political commentary, mostly responding to editorials in relatively mainstream media. Available at http://nielsenhayden.com/electrolite/.

fuckitwasfunny.com: witty, self-deprecating essays on the day-to-day life of a (presumably) young female Brit.

Nuggets of Gold: a diary-type blog about the personal and professional doings of a smart, clever American woman who writes for a newspaper. Available at www.newsgirl.blogspot.com.

filmoculous.com: stripped-down site, with links to cool stories/sites/reports on the Web; the commentary is minimal, but the guy who runs it has excellent taste and is happy to do all the Net trolling that you can't be bothered with.

Kausfiles: astute and idiosyncratic political commentary by Mickey Kaus. Available at www.kausfiles.com.

Best Time to Get Married

The Saturday after Thanksgiving. It may sound like a weird time for a wedding, but Gerald J. Monaghan, president of the Association of Bridal Consultants, believes that it's a date with legs. "Thanksgiving weekend is a dead time for reception halls, so you should be able to get a reasonably good price, and families tend to be together on that weekend anyway," says Monaghan, pointing out that it's not even much of an inconvenience for friends who go out of town for the holiday. "Ordinarily, they'd be coming back by Sunday; so you're only asking people to return home a day earlier for your wedding."

The cheapest month for getting hitched is January, but February runs close behind it and looks like a good alternative to Thanksgiving nuptials. "The end of February is still dead—so you get good rates—and the weather can start to be nice," says Monaghan, pointing out that the premium-priced, mystique-filled June wedding is rooted more in antiquated convenience than in romance. "June was the month after planting and before harvest, so, back in the old days, that made it an appealing time for weddings. Plus, the roads were dry and people liked to get married as soon as they graduated from high school. But those things don't apply anymore. So why should you pay for them?"

Best Time to Play Over Your Head

When you are getting your butt kicked by someone who's better than you—and when losing will have a major consequence for your life. Such was the situation facing poker player Chris Moneymaker during the 2003 World Series of Poker. Moneymaker had never before played in a live poker tournament, and he was poised to take a shot at winning more than two million dollars, as long as he could keep from getting beaten, bluffed, and intimidated by the world's toughest, smartest card sharks.

It was after a day of getting smoked, losing chips, and risking his seat in the tournament that Moneymaker (then a full-time accountant in Nashville, Tennessee) decided to play over his head. "I was furious about having been so outclassed," he says, remembering that big-name players like Johnny Chan and Phil Ivey were routinely pushing him around by making big bets, which Moneymaker was afraid to call. "I'd seen these guys on TV, and I felt like I shouldn't be getting mixed up in hands with them. I figured that they wouldn't be betting with nothing. What I didn't know is that under the right conditions"—particularly against a less seasoned player—"they put their money into the pot and use intimidation, even though they're far from having the best of it."

The next morning, Moneymaker vowed to play better and harder than he ever had before. "I decided not to be scared anymore," he says. "I started gambling and playing more aggressively. I bluffed out Scotty Nguyen [a respected professional poker player and former World Series champ]. I loosened up and began having a good time. Suddenly, I was playing without fear, like I didn't care if I won or lost." The plan worked. Moneymaker went on to snag the Series' first-place prize of $2.5 million.

Best Time to Go to the Dentist

In the morning. According to Dr. Joel Weaver, D.D.S., spokesman for the American Dental Association, there are two reasons for this. First, if you don't spend the entire day worrying about your dental appointment, you'll be more relaxed when you get into the chair. Second, the human body is biologically inclined to contend with stressful scenarios in the morning. "There are compounds released from the adrenal cortex that discharge hormones to help people in dealing with difficult situations," says Weaver. "And the highest levels of these hormones are released just around the time you wake up." Plus, getting drilled in the morning will result in minimized pain after your procedure is completed: "The hormone is just like cortisone, which works as an anti-inflammatory."

However, if you happen to be a smoker, Joel Weaver suggests that you enjoy breakfast and schedule your dental appointment for just before lunch. "Dentists like to treat smokers in the late morning," he says. "We prefer to wait until after they've coughed up their phlegm"—which smokers tend to do during the early-A.M. hours—"before we start working in their mouths."

Best Time to Snap a Paparazzi Picture

"When the bodyguards come at you and tell you to stop shooting, that's the time to make sure you're getting your pictures—because there's probably something interesting going on that the celebrity doesn't want in a magazine," says Randy Bauer, a world-class paparazzo who has stalked the rich and famous on beaches, on streets, and even in hotel rooms. "You want to get them when they are out and about, away from the set, and unguarded. The idea is to show the celebrities for who they really are."

Get the right shot of the right celebrity and it will earn you big bucks from publications like *Star, Us,* and *People.* Such was the case when one of Bauer's associates managed to capture Britney Spears and Colin Farrell mid-smooch at a party in a Chateau Marmont hotel suite in West Hollywood. "A bodyguard saw the flash go off and told our man not to take any more pictures," remembers Bauer. "He put the camera away and said, 'No problem.' By then, though, he already had his shot and they were done kissing. But in case the bodyguard tried to grab the camera from him, we would have been covered: There were a couple guys he could have thrown it to, and they all would have run. The most important thing was to bring back the pictures."

So if you happen to be in the right place at the right time with your Canon point-and-shoot handy—for example, when a very pregnant Kate Hudson is trying to shop incognito in a Malibu grocery store (an all-too-revealing shot of her made the cash registers sing)—Bauer suggests that you act a little heartless: "When other people turn away, because they're too embarrassed to look, or they don't want to bother the celebrity, or they don't want to seem like voyeurs, that's the time to start shooting."

☺ Three Hot Paparazzi Shots and What They Sold For ☺

Subjects: Justin Timberlake and Cameron Diaz

What they're doing: Wading into the Hawaiian surf and kissing.

What the photographer has to say: "Cameron had recently broken her nose, so we were originally going for a shot of the nose. But this was better than what we could have ever imagined. It wound up on the cover of *Us.*"

Ka-ching: $250,000 internationally.

Subjects: Anna Kournikova and Enrique Iglesias

What they're doing: Making out on a waterfront bench in Santa Monica.

What the photographer has to say: "It turned into a peep show: She took her shoes off, straddled Enrique, laid on top of him, and started kissing him. Then *he* got frisky. He stuck his hand right down her pants. We were waiting for them to get undressed."

Ka-ching: $50,000 globally.

Subject: Lara Flynn Boyle

What she's doing: Gorging on McDonald's hamburgers, then showing off her skin-and-bones physique at an L.A. beach.

What the photographer has to say: "We knew she was skinny, but we didn't expect her to look like a refugee with a distended belly,"

Ka-ching: $50,000 domestically.

Best Time to Wait in Line at . . .

. . . the passport agency: Think ahead and you won't need to bother (it'll take six to eight weeks to get a passport via mail), but since the lines are full of people who do wait until the last minute, try to get there early on a fall morning. "It will be busy no matter what, but early in the morning means that the lines will not be too severely backed up," says Nicole Backstrom, senior representative with the passport expediter Passport Express in Providence, Rhode Island. "Fall is the slowest because most people have done their traveling in the summer and don't need passports. Same thing, to a lesser degree, after the holidays—in January and February."

. . . the department of motor vehicles: Midmorning and early afternoon in the middle of the week, fall and winter. There tends to be an early-morning rush that ends at around ten A.M., then it's reasonably quiet till noon, when office workers try to get their cars registered and their licenses renewed during lunch. "On top of that," according to Mike Ward, head of field services for the Oregon State Department of Motor Vehicles, "clerks take lunch at the same time as everyone else. So you have a large number of people coming in when a good percentage of the staff is gone."

Seasonally, summer is busy because people often buy new cars at that time of year and a disproportionate number of students get them for graduation gifts. Adding to long waits is the fact most DMV workers want to take time off during the summer. In terms of monthly cycles, the beginning and end of every month are both busy. "Lots of people wait until the last minute and need to get their cars registered by the thirtieth or the thirty-first. Then there are those who miss the last-day-of-the-month deadline and arrive at the beginning of the next month instead."

. . . **the bank**: Thirty minutes after the doors open, midweek. According to William Ferrence, veteran manager of Boulder Dam Credit Union, in Boulder City, Nevada, and a longtime watcher of lines, "Speedy service is not what you get when we open. You get it after we've taken care of all the people who had been waiting for us to open. Mondays and Fridays are always bad because people are either cashing paychecks or taking care of business that transpired over the weekend."

Best Time to Deliver a Baby

Between April and August. "You don't want to have a baby during winter [or during the months leading into it]," says Dr. Elena Fuentes-Afflick, associate professor in the epidemiology and biostatistics department at the University of California, San Francisco. "That's flu season. You spend a lot of time indoors; germs travel from person to person. If a baby gets a fever during the first two months, the baby gets admitted to the hospital. Winter babies face a higher risk of that happening. And because they can't tell you the degree to which they are sick, we err on the side of caution—especially since a baby who's acting a little funny can have a cold just as easily as he can have the start of meningitis."

What's wrong with September for delivering a baby? "It's the busiest month in the maternity ward, due to behavior during the holiday season, a romantic time, when there is a lot of intimacy between couples."

Best Time to Buy a House

In terms of sheer selection, the best time is when the market is most active, which tends to be from May through July. But you'll pay for the privilege. "Prices are highest then," says H. Bernie Jackson, chairman of the National Association of Real Estate Brokers and a broker with BJR Associates in Baltimore. "Starting in September [the month when price and selection are both somewhat advantageous], you see properties that should have sold but, for some reason, didn't. That's when sellers might be willing to help with closing costs or a down payment."

As winter descends, says Jackson, prices go down (by 3 or 4 percent per month), but selection also withers.

Best Time to Redecorate Your Living Room

In High Point, North Carolina, furniture shows are held twice a year for wholesalers, retailers, and designers. "It's when they go to see the new trends and buy the merchandise that they'll sell over the next six months," says Nancy Golden, an interior designer and the host of DIY Network's *Weekend Decorating*. "In order to make room for the new merchandise, showrooms clear their spaces in April and October. This is the time to buy new furniture, because everything is on sale." However, she cautions, "The timing only applies to floor models and existing pieces in the warehouse, not custom stuff."

Beyond the schedule of the furniture trade, Golden says that there is an emotionally good time for redoing rooms: "After you've gotten back from a special trip to a place where the aesthetic really spoke to you. If you go somewhere and find your comfort level, in terms of art or furniture or design, you shouldn't ignore it. That happened to me after returning from a vacation in the south of France. I experienced a need to readjust my décor so that I'd feel like I was on this trip twelve months of the year. I changed the colors, the fabrics, the artwork, and went from soft contemporary to country French. Soft contemporary suddenly ceased to be who I am."

☺ *Chair Cheat Sheet* ☺

If you're going to redecorate, chairs are key. Tori Golub, a Manhattan-based interior designer who has been featured in *Elle Decor* magazine, provides the ups and downs of finding a cool squat.

Club chair

Characteristics: comfy and plush, always with armrests, deep and roomy, usually upholstered in leather, back is high enough so you can lean your head on it. Enhance the comfort level by getting an ottoman on which to rest your feet.

Upside: great for extended periods of sitting while reading a book or watching TV, very durable, sort of like a sofa for one.

Downside: takes up a lot of space, looks chunky, can dominate a room. Sometimes when salespeople hear that you want a club chair, they will try to sell you something called a chair-and-half. Golub suggests you stay away: "It's too big for one person and not big enough for two."

Slipper chair

Characteristics: scaled-down version of a club chair, without arms, lower and deeper than a standard chair.

Upside: takes up less space than a club chair and is more refined-looking, feels open, but you don't sink into it as much (so there's no embarrassing lunge as you climb out). Put two together with a cocktail table between them and the setting will look very elegant indeed.

Downside: not good for spending an hour watching TV (too uncomfortable)—nowhere to rest your arms.

Tub chair

Characteristics: sort of like a slipper chair with arms, encompasses you without swallowing your entire body, low back contributes to making you feel like you're sitting inside a semicircle.

Upside: works well in the entrance of a room, doesn't feel like it's a big blockade, comfortable without being intrusive.

Downside: not especially popular with furniture producers (or buyers), so your selection will be limited. (On the upside of the downside: All of your friends won't have the same chair.)

Wing chair

Characteristics: has high back and high sides, embraces you, originally designed to protect people from cold breezes.

Upside: no need to talk to anybody when you sit in it (because the chair essentially sequesters you), good for listening in on conversations without other people seeing that you're in the room, modern versions look less stuffy than traditional designs once did.

Downside: too upright and uncomfortable, so big and bulky that it takes up an entire corner of the room.

Chaise longue

Characteristics: the living-room equivalent of a bed, can be contoured and adjusted to fit your body, operates like an extended chair, tends to be tightly upholstered.

Upside: comfortable (especially if you prop yourself on pillows), has a lot of character, can delineate a new seating space, great for filling an empty room.

Downside: need to take off your shoes when you use it, brings out the poseur in people.

Best Time to Pick Up Somebody in a Bar

After you've already gotten one phone number that night. So say tag-team sex columnists Em and Lo.

The thinking here is that you will be extra sure of yourself and not worry about getting shot down—and if you do, who cares? You've got a potential hottie in your back pocket. "Other times might be right after you've gotten a raise, a new haircut, or ran into an ex who is looking terrible," say Em and Lo, authors of *The Big Bang*.

"[Whatever the back story,] you want to be relaxed and natural and confident, which is a good reason for chatting people up during the course of any given night—even if it's just to stay in practice."

The other good time, they say, is when nobody expects it: "Even during the day. People are ready to hear pickup lines at the end of the night, when everyone is drunk and acting confident. It's more flattering to be approached by someone who isn't smashed and immediately needing someone to sleep with." On the flip side, however, after some reconsideration, there's a consensus that it might not hurt to make with the patter after a few martinis: "Sometimes the more successful pickup *is* when people are comfortable about being approached—and they are more comfortable at the end of the night, after they've been out drinking with their friends." In other words, keep trying to pick people up all the time, regardless of the hour and your alcohol level.

Best Time for a Political Debate

Traditionalists might hold to the belief that politics have no place at the dinner table. Bill Maher, host of the now-defunct *Politically Incorrect* and the more recent *Real Time* on HBO, believes that dinnertime is the perfect time for political discourse. In fact, he says, it's second only to an afternoon coffee klatch. "Most of the world is a café society," says Maher. "People sit in cafés and talk and argue about whatever is going on in the world. Go to

London or Paris or Madrid or Baghdad and you'll see people sitting in cafés for hours, drinking coffee, smoking cigarettes, discussing events of the day."

However, do not take this to mean that Maher is fair game for a political debate while he's drinking his brew at Starbucks. "Nobody likes to do in their off time what they do in their job," cautions Maher, making it clear that he enjoys talking politics only when the cameras are rolling or an audience is paying. "Somebody came up to me at a party once and asked what I thought of the Israelis assassinating the head of Hamas. I said, 'No offense, but it's a touchy subject. Everyone has strong opinions about it; we'll have an argument over this, and I'm here to have fun.' It was the equivalent of me approaching Gwen Stefani and asking her to hum a song."

Best Time to Buy Life Insurance

Don't listen to what the life insurance salesmen tell you about needing to start young in order to get a good rate when you're old. The fact of the matter is that you should wait as long as possible, until you definitely need life insurance in order to take care of a spouse or child in the event of your death.

James M. Carson, professor of risk management and insurance at Florida State University, has done the mathematics and knows the facts. "There is no financial advantage to buying life insurance when you are young and don't really need it," Carson says, emphasizing that it will cost you more money over the long haul. "If you are twenty-five years old and want to buy one million dollars' worth of term life insurance that will stay fixed for the next thirty years, you will pay seventy dollars per month for the entire period. If you are forty and want to buy the same policy, but with a fixed fee for fifteen years, it will cost you only around forty-two dollars per month." And the chances of your dying between twenty-five and forty are a lot slimmer than the chances of your dying between forty and fifty-five.

While you're at it, don't let anyone try convincing you that inflation will cause insurance rates to go up over the course of the next fifteen or thirty years. "If anything," says Carson, "the way that mortality statistics keep improving, life insurance costs will keep coming down."

Best Time to Learn to Play Guitar

The late Johnny Ramone, guitarist for the legendary Ramones, didn't pick up his first ax till he was twenty-five years old, out of work, and looking for something to do. Seven months later, he was onstage, bashing out punk rock songs like "Loudmouth" and "Blitzkrieg Bop." He didn't advise waiting till that ripe old age to learn the handful of chords that define his style of play, but he did think there's something to be said for waiting until you know what you want to do with those chords. "It's okay to start playing guitar at the age of twelve—if you want to sound like everyone else," said Johnny. "My advice is that you should wait until you're about sixteen. That way, you're already a rock 'n' roll fan and have some ideas of what you want to do with the music. And you know how you want to look onstage."

That said, it's no surprise that he was also a big believer in dispensing with the playing of other people's songs. To Johnny's way of thinking, the best time to start playing original music is a second after you plug in your guitar for the very first time. He remembered the Ramones' debut practice session, when the band tried to re-create the sixties hit "Yummy Yummy Yummy." It didn't work. "I said, 'How the hell do you play that?'" he recalled. "So we decided to write our own stuff and came up with 'I Don't Wanna Walk Around with You' that day. It wasn't until right before our first gig that I actually had somebody sit down and teach me to play a song written by another group."

☺ Secret of the Ramones' Sound ☺

Arguably the most influential guitarist of the 1970s and 1980s—bands that range from U2 to Nirvana to the Yeah Yeah Yeahs grew up listening to the Ramones—Johnny Ramone said the key to his band's roaring wall of sound was the fact that he never really figured out how to play the guitar properly: None of the Ramones' songs have any up strumming in them. In other words, he only strummed the chords in a downward motion. And there's nothing simple about that. "It's very hard to get through three minutes of down strumming," said Johnny. "But I didn't do it consciously. In fact, I didn't even realize I was doing anything unique."

He insisted that, musically speaking, there was always more to the Ramones than met the eye (or ear). "People made it sound like our songs were so easy," said Johnny, who pointed out that the music, which was disparagingly called "three-chord rock," actually employed *six* chords. "But accomplished guitar players can't do what I did. They can't keep up. I saw Green Day, a great band, and their guitarist couldn't do the down strumming. After three songs, he was exhausted." Johnny chuckled softly, then said, "It's all in the wrist."

Best Time to Refinance a Mortgage

You might figure that it'd be whenever mortgage rates are low. And that's definitely true. But there's also an important issue of relativity. "The percentage differential is the key," says GMAC Mortgage's Barry Habib, a frequent pundit on CNN-FN and CNBC. Habib means that you need to be able to save enough money—based on the size of your mortgage, the percentage you already pay, and the cost of refinancing—to make such an undertaking worthwhile.

You can do a lot of soul-searching and weighing and wondering, or else you can apply a formula he's devised to get a ballpark idea about the financial sense of a refi: Take 125,000 and divide your loan balance into that number. Let's say you have a mortgage of $250,000. It goes into 125,000 half a time. That means you need to be able to save 0.5 percent over your old mortgage for the refinance to be viable.

It's worth remembering that the less you owe on your mortgage, the higher you need your percentage of savings to be. For instance, following Habib's mathematics, if you owe $50,000, you'd want to save at least 2.5 percent (since 50,000 goes into 125,000 2.5 times). "The formulation," he says, "is a way of taking something difficult and turning it into a no-brainer."

Best Time to Write a Scathing Tell-all About Your Famous Boss

After he's dead, after all his friends are dead, and before you forget all the juicy, embarrassing, telling details about the bastard. "You want to wait as long as you can, but you are always running toward this hard wall of losing memory recall," says William Stadiem, coauthor of two such best-selling books (*Marilyn Monroe Confidential,* which is, obviously, about Marilyn Monroe, written with her maid Lena Pepitone; and, more recently, *Mr. S,* about Frank Sinatra, written with his valet, George Jacobs). "You definitely want your subject to be dead, but when the people who know that person are still alive, you run the risk that they won't like how they're portrayed. Then, if they have the resources, there is the possibility that they will hire lawyers and cause great problems for you and your publisher."

In the case of the Sinatra book, Jacobs detailed recollections of his years with the Chairman and then waited patiently. "Most importantly"—after the passing of Sinatra himself—"Sinatra's lawyer, Mickey Rudin, had to be dead," says Stadiem. "Over the years, Rudin had made veiled threats to George that something would happen to him if he wrote a memoir about his ex-boss. And George had seen a lot of violence visited upon people who betrayed Sinatra. So in that instance, the fear wasn't so much that he would get sued as it was that he'd face some kind of Hoboken-style retribution."

Best Time to Sell a Family Business

After you divorce yourself from the looming guilt of quitting on a multigenerational legacy and feel comfortable capitalizing on the fact that the operation is ready to peak—but still has enough upside to make it an appealing proposition for someone else. Whether it's a corner newsstand or a billion-dollar chain of convenience stores, family businesses are inevitably run more on emotion and less on bottom-line savvy than the typical enterprise. But honoring the often apocryphal wishes of Great-Grandpa Benny instead of the cash-out dreams of Great-Grandson Jason can mark the difference between getting out of the enterprise at the optimal moment and hanging in there for no good financial reason.

Wait too long, get too greedy or too emotional, and you'll face diminishing returns in the marketplace (and that, surely, is the last thing Great-Grandpa Benny would have wanted). "If family members don't plan things out, they get forced to sell when the business is going down and thus wind up with less money than they could have gotten otherwise," says Tom L. Ogburn, director of the family business center at Wake Forest University's Babcock Graduate School of Management. Pointing out that only 4 percent of family businesses last through three generations, he adds, "You need to have family meetings where you set values"—philosophical and financial—"and goals for the company."

Because it's so hard to get relatives to concur on much of anything, sales of rising family businesses are most easily timed for those moments when it inarguably makes the only sense: the death of the person running it, a financial need, or an agreement that several people (even those who have no desire to work in the enterprise) should get a share of its value. "With blood involved, it's hard to sell a business—regardless of the timing," warns Ogburn. "You're selling the family's name and the family's tradition, and you have to wonder what that says about you. It's hard to let go of a family business, even if it's being kept going at the deficit of the company's value."

Best Time to Buy Appliances

According to Danielle Johnson, formerly a manager at 4cost.com, a discount retailer of everything from washers and dryers to TVs and stereos, the best time to shop is when everybody else is sick of it. "Right after January 1 is when prices come down," she says. "That's when most retailers want to reduce their inventory."

She points out that the Christmas season is typically the worst time to buy anything, explaining that the supposed holiday markdowns are generally reductions from higher-than-normal prices and aren't really discounts at all.

Looking for electronics? Prior to Thanksgiving, says Johnson, is when you want to hit the stores. "Everyone's aiming to impress their husbands and wives with the latest and greatest for Christmas. And on December 1, the retailers get their hot TVs and stereos. A few weeks before December, they need to get rid of the old stuff—and they do it at a discount to consumers."

⏱ *Beware of SPIFF* ⏱

Ever encounter a salesman who desperately tries to sell you one item over another for no discernible reason? They can be identical in price, identical in features, different only in their midlevel manufacturers—Whirlpool, for example, as compared to General Electric—yet he's making one sound like a piece of junk and the other like the steal of the century.

Chances are that you'll take his advice, and that's fine, as far as it goes, but be aware that he probably receives a SPIFF on the sale. What SPIFF actually stands for is lost to the ages, but the plain truth is that it's a cash incentive for selling a specific brand or model. SPIFFs are provided to salespeople by various manufacturers, and they change all the time, but you can be sure that *something* in the store is top-loaded with a bonus.

This means that the salesman will receive anywhere from five dollars to two hundred dollars (if he's selling you a large-screen TV or high-end refrigerator) when you purchase the specific model that a manufacturer has deemed SPIFF-worthy. And here's the bottom line: The salesman has extra incentive to see you make the purchase, and he ought to be flexible as a Russian gymnast when it comes to negotiating a price.

Best Time to Stick with a Job That You Hate

When you've got a big pile of stock options and the company is moving toward twenty million dollars in annual sales. That's the magic number for going public. "As the twenty-million-dollar figure approaches, people stick around no matter how horrible the working conditions are," says Donald H. MacAdam, author of *Startup to IPO*, who's been involved in managing twenty companies and has shepherded three of them through public offerings. "You normally have 10 to 20 percent of the shares as stock options for employees. Those are used to bring in important people, to give out as bonuses, to use as incentives for keeping people with the company. This is how secretaries suddenly become multimillionaires."

MacAdam explains that it's a beautiful thing to be surrounded by rich people in the making. "The sales department is motivated to get its numbers as high as possible," he says. "You get employees sitting around, continually counting their stock options, brushing up on the rules—often, you can't sell your shares for six months or a year—and all of a sudden everybody is very interested in how the company is doing."

Best Time to Get Punched in the Face

If you're Harmony Korine (writer of *Kids* and *Ken Park*, director of *Gummo* and *Julien Donkey-Boy*), it's when you want to make people laugh. He views a punch in the face—that is, the real thing, not a feigned jab from one stuntman to another, and preferably from an angry stranger—as the ultimate bit of slapstick.

Aiming to prove his point, Korine endeavored to shoot a movie called *Fight Harm*, in which he confronted strangers on the street and agitated them to the point where they felt compelled to punch him. For instance, to get an unsuspecting couple going, Korine smacked a package out of the woman's hands. When the package broke loose, her ordinarily nonviolent husband began attacking Korine. "Obviously, I wasn't completely sober," Korine says. "But at that point in my life, getting beaten up seemed like the right thing to do. I thought I was making the ultimate American comedy." Korine hesitates for a beat. Then he acknowledges, "I was a bit delusional at the time. But in comedy, there is always a victim, and I felt like I was boiling my life down to a giant slip on a banana peel."

So far, Korine—who suffered broken bones and a concussion during the filming—has yet to make the footage public, though he says he is in the process of editing nine fights into a fifteen-minute film. "Whether or not you think it's funny depends on your sense of humor," he admits, citing a segment in which a goaded cabdriver smashes a mandolin on Korine's skull. "I think there's a lot of entertaining banter between me and the people who attack me."

Best Time to Sell Art and Antiques

Time your sale to follow the New York auctions, which take place throughout the year, for specific sorts of collectibles. "All the people involved in collecting converge on New York for those events, mostly at Sotheby's and Christie's, and the sale prices set the tone for what happens across the rest of the United States," says Gary Piattoni, an independent antiques appraiser in Evanston, Illinois, who frequently appears on PBS's *Antiques Roadshow.*

January is the month for Americana auctions, Oriental collectibles are sold in March, and fine-art auctions take place in May and November. If auction prices go up from the previous year (and they usually do), you can raise the price on your item as well. "The great example of this is when Sotheby's had an auction for Andy Warhol's cookie

120

jars in 1988," says Piattoni. "Suddenly, cookie jars were hot and expensive. That auction created a new market and new buyers."

What happens if the auction turns out to be a flop and your hundred-year-old piece of needlepoint proves to be worth less than what it had once been appraised at? "It's certainly no time to sell," says Piattoni. "But it is the time to buy—especially if you think the market is resilient and will bounce back."

Best Time to Go Pro in the Kitchen

When your skills exceed your equipment to the point that cooking becomes frustrating. "You're limiting your menu because you don't have enough burners, you need a second oven so that you can bake a cake while the beef roast is cooking, you're irked because you don't have a convection oven [its fans circulate heat evenly], and nothing is cooking consistently—those are signs that the time is right to turn pro in the kitchen," says Ming Tsai, chef/owner of Blue Ginger restaurant in Wellesley, Massachusetts, and host of the TV show *Simply Ming* (also the name of one of his cookbooks). "If you want to do proper stir-frying in a wok, you need a gas line with 10,000 to 12,000 BTUs, instead of the home-kitchen standard of 3,000. With a typical home stove, it won't get hot enough, and you wind up stewing instead of stirring."

For a serious home cook, Tsai insists, it's virtually impossible to cook a good, halfway ambitious four- or five-course dinner with fewer than half a dozen burners and yards of counter space. But even if such a sprawling, tricked-out kitchen is impossible—financially or logistically—you can improve things by getting good knives and having them sharpened by professionals ("It's necessary for slicing thinly and keeping in flavor," Ming says) and a couple of high-end pots and pans. "One of the key things you want is a heavy-bottomed roasting pan for cooking turkeys and legs of lamb," says Tsai. "You want it to have a heavy bottom so that you can preheat it in the oven, pull it out, drizzle oil on it, throw in your vegetables, and get a great sizzle over which to place the lamb or turkey. It gives you a little carmelization and a nice bed to absorb the juice. And the heavy-bottomed pan keeps searing because it maintains heat."

He considers the current boom in home cooking and concludes, "There are so many people who will cook better and will cook more often with the right equipment. It's a drag when you can't keep your twenty-dollar piece of butterfish from sticking to the bottom of a ten-dollar pan."

✺ How to Fake It Like a Pro ✺

Whether you have a chef's kitchen or not, Ming Tsai offers a few simple ideas for enhancing your meals without breaking the bank:

- Double your oven space by getting an inexpensive freestanding broiler. This will allow you to bake a cake and roast a chicken simultaneously.

- Use a hand blender for finishing sauces and mixing in butter. "However," says Tsai, "don't get the rechargeable one, because it won't put out enough power."

- Invest $125 in a Benriner turning slicer. It's a sharp-bladed gizmo that will let you slice tomatoes as thin as carpaccio and transform whole carrots into strands of orange angel hair. "It justifies us charging twenty-five dollars for a dish, because we can have all kinds of funky garnishes on the plate," says Tsai. "Start frying those garnishes and your meals will look amazing."

- Use squirt bottles. Tsai says, "This is the cheapest way to make things appear professional." Fill them with sauces and decorate plates of food like a Picasso of the kitchen.

Best Time to Find a Tenant

According to Ralph Roberts, the King Kong of real estate brokers, it's the beginning of January.

The thinking here begins with the fact that many people decide to improve their lives after the New Year, and that often includes a housing upgrade. There's another reason, too, says Roberts: "It's best to allow one to four months to rent out a place. And you want to have tenants in there before May"—a time of year that, coincidentally, is when many houses are sold. "By May, renters are making plans for summer, and the last thing they want to do is deal with finding and moving into a new place."

Best Time to Have Sex with 209 People in One Session

After you've already done the deed with 411 strangers. Through the course of a single day, porn star Houston had sex with a total of 620 partners (including a smattering of women) for her group-grope opus *The Houston 500*. "After the first 411, I iced down, smoked a joint, and ate a chicken sandwich; then I took on the remaining 209," Houston says matter-of-factly, clarifying—in case you weren't sure—that it was her vagina that got iced down. "My outer lips were completely swollen, though I was having both vaginal and anal sex. I kept flipping around because I thought it would make things easier."

Initially, Houston was slated to copulate with only five hundred volunteers. "After we hit that number, there were still 120 fans waiting in line, so I said, 'Screw it. I'll finish with the rest of them.'" What can possibly motivate a woman to endure that much penetration? "I wanted to be the biggest porn star in the world," she says, explaining that the movie was shot in a giant warehouse that had been decorated with auto-racing accoutrements. "And I am. This is the best-selling porn film ever."

Asked how one prepares for such an undertaking,

Houston offers a halfway credible response: "I did Kegel exercises, drank a lot of water, and stayed away from liquor." She points out, however, that the physical challenge was not the most daunting part of her record breaking stunt. "Most people couldn't handle it mentally. I had sex for ten hours that day and will never regret doing it."

Best Time for a Mediterranean Cruise

When there is the whiff of global tension that makes international travel look like Russian roulette. "Mediterranean cruises are particularly sensitive to unrest around the world"—even if it has nothing to do with your specific Mediterranean destination, says Nancy Kelly, president of Kelly Cruises, a travel agency in Oak Brook, Illinois, which was rated one of America's top cruise specialists. "People consider the Mediterranean to be exotic, and if travelers are uncomfortable with leaving the United States, well, then, business over there drops deeper than in other places."

October and November are particularly good counterintuitive months for Mediterranean cruises. The weather may be a little bit iffy, but the crowds are down (summertime is brutal in terms of the crush of European tourists) and so are the fares. Especially if there's friction in, say, the Middle East. "People forget that the Mediterranean, which includes Turkey, also encompasses Italy and France," continues Kelly. "But there are some tourists who are drawn to the fear factor. They'll go to a destination"—

and this holds especially true for the Mediterranean, which is basically safe—"precisely because other people are afraid to go there."

While it's the kind of trip that might enhance your coolness standing as a hearty traveler, the real draws are the deep price cuts. "Great deals can be found out there all the time these days. Discounts (depending on the public's collective nervousness) go from 20 to 50 percent below published rates."

Best Time to Renovate Your Home

Kermit Baker, director of the remodeling futures program at Harvard University's Joint Center for Housing Studies, says you want to do home repairs when contractors' business is the slowest. That makes them hungry for work and likely to finish quickly (so they can get paid). Considering Baker's advice, winter is a good time because big-money exterior projects, such as home additions and refinishings, never happen in freezing-cold conditions.

January, in particular, is when contractors tend to be most available and most negotiable—they're not yet booked with warm-weather work and have holiday bills to pay.

If your own timing is flexible, Baker offers an interesting option: "Give the contractor an opportunity to do the work whenever he is not busy with other jobs. You can negotiate a good price, but make sure that once he commits to doing it, he will do it, to completion, within a solid block of time."

⏱ *Men Without Licenses* ⏱

Hire an architect and you can be confident that the person is licensed and operating within certain preordained guidelines. Hire a general contractor and you may be getting a madman with a hammer and no one who's accountable—only twenty-eight states offer licensing for contractors, and the standards vary wildly; in Iowa, for instance, there are no requirements at all, while in California contractors must take an examination and prove their financial solvency. Maybe this helps explain why home-improvement services—which tend to be owned or overseen by contractors—rank number one on the list of consumer complaints issued by the National Association of Consumer Agency Administrators.

Even if your state does not keep its contractors on a short leash, though, you can reduce the chances for bad surprises by knowing as much as possible about the people you hire and what to expect from them.

Beyond getting references, Wendy Weinberg, executive director of the National Association of Consumer Agency Administrators, suggests visiting a job in progress. "That will give you an idea as to whether or not you really want these particular workers in your home," says Weinberg. "You can wind up with beer cans scattered around the living room, rough-talking people within earshot of your young kids, and a degree of sloppiness that extends beyond the work area. Plus, you'll get an indication as to what all that dust and dirt will do to the rest of your house."

Best Time to Get an Invention Patented

Great ideas need to be protected—quickly. Mark Farson, a Florida-based patent facilitator who's worked on snaking more than two thousand would-be patents through the system, advises that you get your ideas to the patent office just after January 1. "They push everything through at the end of the year," says Farson, explaining that a patent-pending request has to be answered (but not approved or rejected) within the calendar year that the application goes in and that you ordinarily get a response after eight to ten weeks. "If you apply in January, they have more time to look at it and are more likely to give you a fair shot," Farson says, because the patent office's employees are now working with a clean slate, as all the previous year's requests have moved on to the next stage or been rejected.

Even if you have a fair shot, however, Farson acknowledges that getting a patent is by no means a slam dunk. "Out of ten inquiries, only two get approved for a final decision. And from there, only 5 percent actually get the patent."

Best Time to Stop Renting

The correct response to this is "as soon as possible." The quicker you stop paying someone else's mortgage (that is, your landlord's) and start paying your own, the better off you'll be. But the truly best time for making the leap from renter to owner is when you can afford it.

According to Gawana Greenleaf, who works as a housing counselor with the nonprofit Consumer Credit Counseling Service of Greater Atlanta, "That happens when your debt-to-income ratio is no more than 28 percent." Huh? "You should not spend more than 28 percent of your gross income on a mortgage." In other words, if you earn sixty thousand dollars per year (or five thousand per month), your monthly mortgage payments should clock in at fourteen hundred dollars or less.

And there is a second component to Greenleaf's rule: "Total debt, including your housing payments, should not exceed 36 percent of your monthly income." So, if we take that same sixty thousand dollars per year, and you buy a house with a monthly mortgage of fourteen hundred dollars, your credit-card debt, car loan, and so on should be less than four hundred dollars per month. Ideally, you would want your total debt—including mortgage, credit cards, and loans—to be eighteen hundred dollars per month or less.

Speaking in the grim tone that she uses on her money-strapped clients, Greenleaf says, "The more debt you have, the more you eat into the amount of house you can afford."

Best Time to Seek a Divorce

According to Henry Berman, managing partner of Berman Bavero Frucco & Gouz, P.C., the best time to get a divorce is when your marriage is the least complicated: no kids, no mortgage, limited years of bitterness. "When you get to a point where you agree that the marriage is over and it's clear that a business decision must be made, that is when a divorce will be the cheapest and quickest," he says, adding that the procedure should be rational rather than emotional. "That means you do it before starting an extramarital affair"—or at least before your spouse finds out about it.

Best Time to Hire a Landscaper

Those who listen to Roger Cook, landscaping guru of *This Old House* and owner of Burlington, Massachusetts–based K&R Tree & Landscape, abide by what he calls the "two-week rule": If you have a job to do and haven't managed to complete it in two weeks, call in a professional, because, odds are, you'll never get around to doing it yourself.

And, says Cook, there is good reason for this. "Usually the unappealing jobs involve moving a lot of material, maybe for a raised flower bed or walkway. Most home-owners get stuck doing it with a wheelbarrow. It physically kills them and takes the fun out of gardening. Contract a landscaper to do the heavy lifting and get the grade right. Let them do the hard work. Then you do the planting. That's the rewarding part."

Cook is also a big believer in having a master plan for your garden—that is, a specific schedule outlining what you'll plant when. He suggests consulting with a landscaper, recording the information, and devising a plan you can stick with. "Otherwise, you're planting the wrong things in the wrong places at the wrong times, and it can lead you to tear up a lot of flowers."

⊕ *Mystery of the Murdered Mums* ⊕

A month ago, your landscaper planted new shrubs in your front yard. They looked great for a day. Now they look like a wheat field. The landscaper blames you for failing to water them enough. You blame the landscaper for buying bush-league bushes. Who's right? It doesn't matter—the plants are dead, and don't expect your landscaper to refund your money cheerfully.

Jeff Herman, co-owner of Herman Brothers Landscaping in Fairlawn, New Jersey, says landscapers get no money-back guarantee from nurseries on the plants and shrubs they buy for home owners: "They figure that the landscaper ought to know what he's doing."

Still, that doesn't mean your landscaper can't provide you with some protection. While you'll have little chance to get a refund on such things as rose-bushes (they're prone to bugs) or ground cover (for instance, ivy, which will die quickly if not watered), you should demand some kind of payback from the landscaper if it's obvious you properly cared for the plantings. "Show your landscaper the grass around the dead plant," advises Hugo Davis, past president of the Kentucky Nursery and Landscape Association, a trade organization for landscapers and nursery owners. "If it's green and thriving, well, then you did all the watering you needed to do."

Best Time to Be Dragged
Through the Gossip Columns

When you're a young nobody and are desperately trying to promote yourself. Once you're established, negative media attention can destroy your hard-won credibility—think Pee Wee Herman and Michael Jackson—but for someone who's yet to land on the public's radar, even the most embarrassing press is weirdly desirable. "It can actually help a burgeoning career, even if it's horrible stuff," says Richard Johnson, whose "Page Six" column in the *New York Post* is America's must-read gossipfest. "It keeps people thinking about you and talking about you"—even if it's simply because you've done something that is way too outrageous or obnoxious for anyone to forget, try as they may. "Notoriety has helped Paris Hilton a lot. There are people who believe she orchestrated the release of that sex tape for the simple reason that it would get everybody talking about Paris—and it did."

Best Time to Look for a Job

August and December. Linda Segal, principal with an executive recruiting firm called the McCormick Group, isn't 100 percent sure why these months tend to be strong for her, but she says that they are. She figures that it might have to do with department heads wanting to hire prior to the beginning of the new year. "And for a lot of companies," says Segal, "the fiscal year begins in September. But if you want a government job, keep in mind that it starts in October."

More generally, says Segal, the other good time to find a job is when you currently have one. And it's not only because you radiate a less-than-desperate aura. There's a practical reason as well. "You have time to do the research and determine which field you want to go into and how to get there," she says. "It gives you an opportunity to network and find out how to break into a new company while paying your bills"—not to mention that you also have the cash flow for picking up lunch tabs and the wherewithal for a quick trip to a potential employer's headquarters if need be. "The problem with finding a job when you're out of work is that you never have the time to look for the career change that you probably need." And you may need to make that change in order to remain happily employed for the long haul.

Best Time to Throw in the Towel

As cornerman for his son "Sugar" Shane Mosley, Jack Mosley hasn't had to bail out of too many fights. Shane Mosley's record, after all, is 39–3. However, Jack's seen his share of fights stopped from the other side of the ring. Throwing in the towel—in boxing or in life—is a delicate operation. Mosley says you need to find the moment where the likelihood of winning is a long shot and injury is becoming an increasingly likely outcome.

Asked to quantify the best time to quit, he says, "It's when your fighter is getting hit three to one—that is, taking three punches for every one that he throws. On top of that, he's not strong, nothing he does seems to work, and, technically, he's not sound enough to beat the other guy. The tricky thing is to figure out when the other guy is getting lucky and when he is truly outfighting your man—because there's always a chance that your guy can bounce back. But if he is getting hurt or having equilibrium problems, there won't be any bouncing back. That's the time to end the fight."

Early on in "Sugar" Shane Mosley's boxing career, papa Jack had plenty of opportunities to mull the question as to whether or not the towel should be thrown in. He developed a trick for buying time while making the decision. "After Shane got knocked down, I had him get up and run around the ring until his head cleared," recalls Jack. "That way, he wasn't going to get hit, and I had a chance to see whether or not he was really hurt. I figure you need a 50 percent or better chance of winning in order to warrant going on. Otherwise, why bother? You might get in a lucky haymaker, but chances are that things will only become worse—and your fighter will wind up getting himself injured."

Best Time for a Catnap

The Spanish have it right, according to Dr. Carl E. Hunt, director of the National Center on Sleep Disorder Research: "In terms of our circadian rhythms, there is a low that occurs in the early to midafternoon time frame. Data suggests that naps of fifteen minutes to one hour"—particularly if taken during that period—"are restorative. Sleep more than an hour and there will be increased downtime before you can become productive again." However, Hunt is quick to point out that "if you are getting enough sleep during the night, then you should not need a nap in the afternoon."

☺ *World-Famous Nappers* ☺

Next time someone hints that you're lazy for catching Z's in the middle of the day, whip out this list of overachievers who thrived on the rejuvenation of afternoon naps.

Thomas Edison: A frequent napper, he believed that a population of night sleepers indicated the regression of our civilization.

Napoléon Bonaparte: He claimed to sleep only four hours per night, though he napped regularly during the day. Those around him believed that he low-balled his nighttime sleeping hours. Historians surmise that fatigue may have hindered his ability to lead an army.

Winston Churchill: He rarely slept through the night during World War II. Churchill compensated by taking four two-hour naps per day, and he insisted that the siestas left him feeling perfectly well rested.

Salvador Dalí: The abstract painter frequently napped while sitting in an easy chair. He held a spoon in his hand and placed a china plate between his feet. The reasoning was this: As soon as Dalí dozed off, he'd drop the spoon, which would hit the plate and wake him up. In that split second between slumber and wakefulness, Dalí hoped to capture what he called "the snapshot of thought." Whether or not this actually panned out remains unclear.

Now for a sneaky person who didn't nap but also made it look like he didn't sleep: **Joseph Stalin** He claimed that he routinely worked through the night. The truth is that Stalin did nothing more than simply keep his office lights burning twenty-four/seven. Not surprisingly, the cruel dictator was never challenged on this bit of obvious fabrication.

Best Time to Terminate Psychotherapy

Like a lot of things that have to do with seeing a shrink, the answer to this one is slippery—and less obvious than it sounds. "Think about what motivates you to spend the time and money and endure the inconvenience of going into therapy," suggests Dr. Phillip Freeman, a training and supervising psychoanalyst who taught a termination seminar at Boston Psychoanalytic Institute. "At a point, it stops feeling worth it. And when that feeling derives from the fact that you're not suffering enough to continue with therapy, it's time to start thinking about termination." The doctor hesitates for a beat. Then he softly adds, "But you need to be suspicious of the mood for termination. Thinking you're prepared to be done with therapy is the time to examine *why* you are thinking that. Maybe it is time to stop. Or maybe the thought was motivated by something else entirely."

Okay. Let's say you and your doctor decide that you are indeed fully ready to cease therapy and a parting of the ways is in order. Set a date for termination and expect to spend three months in the wind-down process. Doctors and patients often choose to terminate in the summer, just before August, when shrinks typically take vacations. The thinking is that this will create a natural bridge between life with and without therapy. However, according to Stephen Firestein, supervising analyst at the Psychoanalytic Institute at New York University Medical Center and author of *Termination in Psychoanalysis,* "Summer is not the best time to do it. Patients tell me that when they end at the start of the summer recess, the termination doesn't really kick in till after Labor Day—when they would have previously been going back to see their doctors." So the bridge winds up being more like a diving board. "A better time to terminate is when the therapist is going to be around for a while"—sometime between January and May, for instance. "That way, the immediate, unexpected responses to stopping therapy can be dealt with. You just never know what will come up."

Best Time to Enter the Stock Market

Immediately—regardless of what the market is doing at any given moment. At least that's the strategy espoused by Bryan Olson, vice president at the Schwab Center for Investment Research. "I'm not sure what will happen with stocks over the next week or month," says Olson, "but I am confident that over the next five or ten years the market will go up."

That's the broad advice. More specifically, certain types of stocks have their seasons. "Fall and early winter are the best times to buy small-cap stocks, because they usually take off in January," continues Olson. "The other time to invest is at the bottom of a bear market. But that's not easy to time, and it's not something you want to miss. If you look at the person who's in at the bottom of a bear market, compared to somebody who just misses it and jumps in a month later, the person who was in at the bottom earns 13 percent more over the next twelve months. One other thing to keep in mind is that when you have three down years in a row, the market almost always pops back in the fourth year. And the way you want to play that is with growth stocks. As the market comes back, they should do the best."

Best Time to Get Pregnant

The day of ovulation and the five days leading up to it. "If you wait one day after ovulation, you have a very poor chance of getting pregnant," says Allen Wilcox, senior investigator with the National Institute of Environmental Health Sciences. "The egg dies if it is not fertilized within a precise time frame. The peak is twenty-four to forty-eight hours prior to ovulation."

Unfortunately, as Wilcox emphasizes, most women don't know when they're ovulating—or about to. "Some women have symptoms, which may or may not be accurate," he says. "The best way is to check your cervical mucus. You do an actual internal exam on yourself (using a speculum) to see the character of the mucus." Fertile mucus tends to be slippery and on the clear side, like an egg white, as opposed to white and creamy.

You can also monitor fertility by using an ovulation-predictor kit, or else employ the old-fashioned hit-and-miss approach to baby making—unpredictable but inarguably lots of fun. "Most people have intercourse often enough," says Wilcox, "that there's room for error, and they still get it right."

Best Time to Plant a Garden

Depends on what you're planting. Maureen Gilmer, host of *Weekend Gardening* on cable TV's DIY Network, explains that planting seasons can run through much of the calendar year. If, for instance, you're doing trees and shrubs, it's best to plant in the fall. "That way," she says, "they get somewhat established before the cold sets in. Then when spring comes, they are already adjusted to the new location and ready to put on growth and burst into bloom. Plant them in the spring and there will be a lag period before they bloom."

Flowers like zinnias, petunias, and marigolds require warm soil in order to grow. If you plant these too soon, the seeds won't sprout or the plants will rot and get eaten by bugs. Instead, Gilmer suggests, hold off till the last frost date—generally sometime in May or June—before planting. But if you simply can't wait to get your hands dirty, develop a taste for snapdragons and primroses. Those go into the ground a couple weeks before the last frost day.

Vegetables, on the other hand, should be planted either in spring or fall—both of which are growth seasons with moderate temperatures. The best time for planting strawberries and raspberries is in March or April (as soon as the ground is soft for strawberries; wait until late March for raspberries). In both cases, the goal is to get them well established before the high temperatures kick in.

☯ *Bloom-time Cheat Sheet* ☯

Different flowers bloom at different times of the year. Knowing when to expect a beautiful bud instead of a sharp stick takes a lot of guesswork, and disappointment, out of gardening.

Maureen Gilmer says there's no reason why you shouldn't have a beautiful-looking garden for most of the year. "The vast majority of plants bloom in the spring," she acknowledges. "But the trick is to get the kinds of plants that will also bloom in the heat of summer and the cool of fall." Here's Gilmer's guide to having buds when it seems like you shouldn't:

Plantings that bloom in the fall: Astors, black-eyed Susans, chrysanthemums, maple trees, sumacs ("they have beautiful flowers in the fall"), *Hydrangea paniculata* ("the variety is Tardiva, and it will bloom into November if you live in the eastern part of the United States"), and ornamental grasses.

Plantings that bloom in the summer: Blazing star, echinacea, black-eyed Susans, coreopsis (also known as tick seed), Russian sage, phlox, roses, pincushion flowers, and euphorbia.

Best Time to Restructure Debt

When you're in the most trouble and the market is in the worst shape. It's the time when banks will be willing to make deals and soften their terms, because they'd rather do that than see you default and declare bankruptcy. Just ask Donald Trump. In 1991, as New York real estate appeared to be on the verge of collapse, he was as well—with a two-billion-dollar debt and limited revenue on the immediate horizon. "That was when I totally renegotiated the debt"—to defer payments and receive additional millions—"but it is always unpleasant and unfortunate," says Trump, who, as a condition of the restructuring, was forced to keep his personal spending down to a mere $450,000 per month. "In my case, the banks liked me, they respected me, they liked the jobs that I did. And they do business with me today. Declaring bankruptcy would have been the easy way out. But if I'd done that, I wouldn't have been able to get loans in the future and wouldn't have the wealth that I do right now."

Best Time to Listen to Your Body

Our bodies have internal clocks, and those clocks tell us when we are best suited for certain activities—based on biological and cognitive efficiency. These are known as circadian rhythms, and they signify the physiologically best times in which to do everything.

Michael Smolensky, director of the Chronobiology Center at Herman Hospital in Houston and coauthor (with Lynne Lamberg) of *The Body Clock Guide to Better Health,* breaks down the times of day that are most ideal for specific tasks.

Morning
- Having sex (testosterone peaks)
- Eating a large meal (body temperature is low, so calories are burned to provide energy and are less likely to be stored as fat)
- Taking an anti-inflammatory or allergy pill (inflammation, rheumatoid arthritis, and allergy sensitivity all peak in the morning)
- Relaxing (heart attacks and strokes are most common in the early morning)

Afternoon and Evening
- Doing math
- Tolerating alcohol (truest in the early evening)
- Eating a gourmet meal (your taste buds reach peak sensitivity at night)
- Taking a daily aspirin for prevention of a heart attack (the stomach lining is least vulnerable to the side effects of aspirin)

Best Time for a Pap Smear

Ten to twenty days after your period ends and after two days of celibacy. "The ten to twenty days will bracket a woman far enough away from when she might be bleeding," says Dr. George Sawaya, associate professor in the department of obstetrics and gynecology at the University of California at San Francisco. "And the reason we don't want her to have had intercourse before coming in is because it may cause inflammation that will interfere with the Pap smear." He also cautions against douching or inserting a tampon prior to a Pap smear: "We want to get a representative sample of cells, and they might be disturbed or washed away by either of those two things."

Best Time to Deal with an Obnoxious Neighbor

We've all had to contend with these inconsiderate screwballs: the guy with the dog that won't stop barking, the woman who thinks everyone loves listening to her *Godspell* sound track at top volume, the couple who argues like a bad version of the Bundys. The good news, according to Cora Jordan, an attorney in Oxford, Mississippi, and the author of *Neighbor Law: Fences, Trees, Boundaries and Noise,* is that the no-goodniks next door probably don't realize how annoying they are. The bad news is that you need to tell them.

Choosing the right time for a blunt conversation will relieve some of the inherent tension. "Best time to deal with a loud party is when there is a second loud party," says Jordan, explaining that the first one might be a rare event, which won't happen again for another year or two. "Call the neighbor during that second party and ask him to quiet down. But if there's a loud argument, wait till the next day to say something. Whoever's arguing is already hot, and your asking him to stop will only get him more worked up. I advise people to have the post-argument conversation in a neutral spot—on the sidewalk, outside of your homes."

And if it's a barking dog you need to contend with, lodge the complaint while the pooch is woof-woofing at its loudest. "Most people are horrified to find that they are bad neighbors. So if you approach them with a good attitude and a bona fide problem, well, it's hard for them to do anything but resolve the situation to your satisfaction."

☺ Worst Way to Deal with an Obnoxious Neighbor—Regardless of the Time ☺

Pulitzer Prize–winning novelist Richard Ford remembers an ugly incident from his gin-drinking days in New Orleans: "I got into a serious fistfight with an antiques-dealing neighbor named Clyde over a dog that had been barking for a month. I saw Clyde standing in front of his house, going through his mail, and I politely asked him to do something about his dog barking. He looked at me and said, 'No. My dog can bark all he wants to bark, anytime he wants to bark, and you can't do anything about it.' Then I knocked the mail out of his hand." Punches were exchanged, and the police were called. Ford ended up handcuffed on Bourbon Street. Clyde went to the hospital with what appeared to be a broken nose. The dog, presumably, continued to bark.

This story would be a pretty good one if it ended right here, but Ford offers a memorable kicker: "A year later, I was walking past Clyde's antiques store. I went in there and told him that he might remember me. He showed me the big scar on his nose that I had left. I apologized for whatever part I had played in that incident. Then he told me that because I'd kicked his ass, I'd probably saved his life. They took him to the hospital and discovered that he had very high blood pressure and treated the condition immediately. It was hard to take that as a compliment, but we became friendly after that talk."

Best Time to Give Bad News

When the person you're breaking it to is in reasonably good spirits and you have a bit of positive info that will help to temper the negative—you know: "I lost the big account, but the guy who runs our second-biggest account is increasing his order." "You want to dilute it a little bit," says John Challenger, CEO of Challenger, Gray & Christmas, an outplacement firm based in Chicago. "While you want to address what you did, and not skirt around it, be clear that the bad thing is in the past and that you hope to move toward forgiveness."

Challenger suggests that you choose a time when you're feeling physically strong ("Giving bad news can be debilitating," he says) and won't be interrupted by ringing phones. "But don't let it go for too long," he advises. "The longer you let bad news fester, the worse it gets, and the harder it is to resolve." Challenger, who's orchestrated more than his share of subtle job shifts and balls-to-the-wall firings, adds, "Most people leave jobs"—voluntarily or otherwise— "not because they have done something incredibly wrong. Usually, it's due to ongoing conflicts that slowly cause the boss to sour and relationships to deteriorate. One way to prevent that from happening is to address problems in good faith and remind your boss that it's not the norm."

Best Time to Pose Nude for *Playgirl*

So you're a guy whose twenty-year-old girlfriend just did a shoot with *Playboy*. You're the same age as she is, and every bit as good-looking? Mazel tov. But don't think it'll necessarily get you into the pages of *Playgirl*. "The best time for a guy to pose for us is when he is totally in shape and over forty," says *Playgirl* editor in chief Michelle Zipp. While plenty of young bloods cavort between the magazine's covers, Zipp points out that older gents are what subscribers want and what editors search for. "Readers write in to us all the time, complaining that we have too many young guys in the magazine. They want men who are older, show chest hair, and have found their way in the world. But these guys are the hardest to find. There's a limited pool of older guys who are in appropriate shape and willing to pose."

Zipp adds that the on-set vibe varies wildly between the young hunks and her forty-plus studs. "Young guys in the studio feel that they have something to prove; they're strutting around, thinking they're so hot, wanting everyone to look at them," says Zipp. "The older men seem to be there more for themselves. They're proud of their bodies, and this is a way for them to be appreciated."

Best Time for Your Rich Uncle to Die

In 2010. That is when, for one year only, the federal government will repeal estate taxes. That's right. No taxes on any money you inherit for the entire year. However, if Uncle Rich happens to kick it during the wee hours of January 1, 2011, expect to pay taxes on every dollar after the first million. "It's been called the 'Throw Mama from the Train Act,'" half-jokes Joel Friedman, senior fellow with the Washington, D.C.–based watchdog organization Center on Budget and Policy Priorities. "The George W. Bush administration wanted to repeal all estate taxes— permanently. But they couldn't get away with doing it in one shot. So it's being phased in slowly, over a period of ten years. Then, in 2010, people behind the move can say they repealed those taxes and try to keep it that way permanently." But don't get your hopes up. "It's an artificial construct and will be difficult to maintain—if only because this country can't afford it."

Best Time to Pig Out with a High-Cholesterol Dinner

Right after a couple of calorie-burning hours of basketball or tennis—as long as you play a few times per week. "Exercise on a regular basis impacts your cholesterol profile," says Dr. William Kraus, associate professor in Duke University's department of medicine and coauthor of a study on the relationship between cholesterol and exercise. "Muscles that you exercise need fatty acids and triglycerides for fuel. The muscle processes fatty particles that go with cholesterol. Theoretically, then, after you exercise, you process the cholesterol more efficiently." Told that it's easy to imagine there'd be a dip in cholesterol counts among those who exercise due to the simple fact that they probably are more careful about what they eat, Kraus does not concur. "It surprises me a bit, but, generally, exercise does not induce any change in dietary patterns."

🕐 How to Cook a Restaurant-Style Steak, So You Can Enjoy Your Fabulously High-Cholesterol Meal at Home 🕐

When you want that fatty fix, you go to the butcher, buy the best steak possible, and throw it into the broiler or onto a hot skillet. You wind up with a good slice of cooked beef, but not a great one. How come? Probably because your cookware can't get hot enough to create the char that holds in juices and adds the crunchy, smoky, textured flavor that defines a perfect black-and-*bleu* restaurant-prepared steak. Tony Tammero, executive chef at New York–based Palm steak house, has felt that frustration while cooking at home. He's devised a solution:

1. Buy a couple of sixteen-ounce USDA prime New York strip steaks, trimmed so that there is just a little bit of fat rimming the meat. Brush the meat with olive oil.

2. Fire up your stove and place a frying pan on a high flame so that it gets superhot. When you see a little smoke rising from the cooking surface, you're there.

3. Place the steaks in the pan, remove the pan from heat, and rest an identical pan on top of the pan with the steaks in it, using the second pan as a cover. Keep it on there for three minutes before carrying the steaks out a back door or onto the

fire escape, where you remove the top pan and release the smoke (lest you set off smoke detectors and leave the air in your kitchen chokingly funky).

4. Remove the steaks to a plate, season both sides with salt and pepper, get the pan superhot again, and repeat the process on the uncooked sides.

5. Once both pieces of meat have been cooked, let them sit for at least thirty minutes. Then, just before serving, throw the steaks into an oven that's been preheated to 425 degrees Fahrenheit. Keep them in there for two minutes if you want your steaks rare, eight minutes if you want them medium.

And, voilà, a perfectly cooked, restaurant-worthy dinner for two. "When your other half doesn't want you to smoke up the kitchen, you have to devise something," says Tammero, as a way of explaining the inspiration for this technique. "It gives you a fantastic steak, and it really works. Perfect this, and you will never cook steak another way again."

Best Time to Change

Rock 'n' roll star Lou Reed has made a career out of being a chameleon—in one incarnation, he shaved a Maltese cross into his closely shorn hair; in another, he resembled a suburban gearhead with bulging muscles,

Harleys in the garage, and a pinball addiction. So Reed knows about changing.

He believes that the best time to transform is when you don't see it coming. "I *feel* it," says Reed of the moment when he makes a change in his music, his sexual persona, his look. "I can think all I want about what I should do, but I act on instinct. And I just try to stay out of the way. I've done things after being told by other people that I was making the worst move any human being can possibly make." Springing immediately to mind is his mid-1970s release of *Metal Machine Music*—a double album comprised of nothing but symphonic-sounding feedback. Naysayers of a more recent vintage might have doubted his decision to do a CD based on "The Raven." "But it turned out that the other people were wrong," insists Reed. "There's nothing calculated about me. The modus operandi is never 'This will be the smart thing to do.' The modus operandi is 'This will be the fun thing to do,' or 'This will be the beautiful thing to do.' Then something happens."

Best Time to Take Credit

The trick here is to time it so that taking credit doesn't look like showboating but still conveys the right point to the right people.

Ken Blanchard, corporate business consultant and author of *The One Minute Manager,* suggests that you do it consistently and routinely. "You ought to make sure you have regularly scheduled weekly or biweekly meetings with bosses and people who are important—and you use those meetings to take the credit," says Blanchard. "People are interested in hearing what you are excited about." And you need to couch your credit-taking in that context, he advises. "But you should balance credit with concern, so that people don't think you run around and do nothing but spread good news about yourself."

Best Time for an On-the-Job Romance

When you can keep a secret. Joni Johnston, president of workrelationships.com and a clinical psychologist, so strongly believes that the complications of mixing dating with working outweigh the long-term rewards—that is, the likelihood of marrying your interoffice Romeo—that she advises dodging it all together.

But since, as Woody Allen can tell you, the heart wants what the heart wants, avoidance may be impossible. In that instance, she suggests discretion and insists that you date somebody from outside your department. "Even if you don't breathe a word of the relationship to anybody—which is extremely difficult—chances are that it will leak out at some point," says Johnston. "But if you don't let comments and a little bit of teasing get to you, then, fine, it can work." That's as long as things are going well.

The real problem isn't the romance; it's the end of the romance. What happens when the relationship fizzles and you are forced to see the person you dumped or, even worse, the one who dumped you, every single day? "With the high-pitched emotions of a failed romance, it's impossible to get work done," states Johnston. "Things become even worse when one person adamantly wants to continue the relationship. And gasoline really gets poured on the fire when he or she starts dating someone else in the office."

Bottom line: It inevitably starts to have an impact on job performance. "No matter how liberal a company is, the boss won't be enthusiastic about postrelationship friction," says Johnston. "I've seen people quit perfectly good jobs because they were head over heels in love with someone and couldn't stand to see that person every day. It can be torturous."

Best Time to Sell Your House

More homes get sold in the spring and summer than during any other time of year. In terms of the lifetime of your home, top-selling real estate broker Ralph Roberts suggests that you wait ten years after buying it. "That way, you'll be pretty sure to have doubled the price, and you'll have paid off enough of your principal to enjoy a nice windfall on top of it," he says. "At the very least, you want to live in the house for two years. Any less than that and you'll wind up paying capital gains tax on your profits. That is not what you want to do."

Additionally, waiting a good chunk of time (say, ten years) allows you to have enough equity in the home that you can offer it at a competitive price. "Only 50 percent of houses put up for sale actually sell," adds Roberts, pointing out that there is another timing issue—albeit one that may be as difficult to predict as a stock market dip. "You need to orchestrate things so that there's not much competition from other people, with similar houses for sale, in your neighborhood."

☉ *A Secret from the Real Estate Trenches* ☉

Brokers like to make it sound as if their fees are engraved in stone, but that's rarely the case—especially in a brisk market, where the middlemen fiercely scramble for properties they can unload fast. One broker in the Southwest says that in a brisk market he will happily lower his fee by a full percentage point. "There's so much competition for the best houses that a reduced fee gives me an advantage over my competitors," he says.

Indeed, advises the realtor, who asked not to be named, home sellers should shop around for the most attractive brokers' fees. He offers these scenarios for bringing them down: "If somebody's willing to commit to me for selling one place and buying another, I give a discount. If you're in a particularly desirable neighborhood, with a house that will sell quickly and require minimal effort on my part, I'm negotiable. But with some brokers, especially if they're desperate for inventory, all you need to do is ask, and they'll lower their commissions."

Best Time to Pick Up a Lunch or Dinner Tab

Socially speaking, it's bad form to invite someone out for a meal and neglect to pay (even if your guest is megarich). Moreover, if the person happens to be doing you a favor in the process, well, then you absolutely must dig out a credit card and banish the thought of going splitsies. Marjorie Brody, career expert and etiquette columnist for BusinessWeek Online, recently found herself on the sticky end of such a transaction: "Somebody invited me to lunch because she wanted to pick my brain. I don't usually do this, but it was a friend of a friend. The bill came, she looked at it, and said that we should split it. Do you think I will ever help this person again?" Uhm, one would guess not.

Had they gone to the Four Seasons, a power-lunch haven in New York City, there would have been no splitting. Waiters there receive strict orders to present the check to whoever made the reservation and to refuse payment from any guests. In case you're eating elsewhere, however, and your boss, client, or colleague insists on paying a tab that you ought to pick up, Brody suggests heading them off at the pass: "If you're a woman and there seems to be a gender issue, tell the other person that it's on the company. If you have invited a superior out for lunch, make sure that you give your credit card to the maître d' ahead of time. If you sit down and sense that the waiter doesn't know who is the invitee and who is the host, you might want to say, 'Let my guest order first.'"

But what happens when you and a colleague mutually decide to eat lunch together and there is no clear-cut host? "If you want the other person to owe you one, pick up the tab. It is never an error to be generous."

Best Time to Fight Back

Your temptation might be to do it immediately, while the wound is still fresh. Not a good idea. Miriam Browning, former deputy chief information officer for the Department of the Army and currently a principal with the corporate consulting firm Booz Allen Hamilton, suggests, "You really need a cool-down period—even if it's only a couple of hours. The worst thing you can do is fire off an e-mail, or make an angry telephone call"—or, even worse, throw a punch—"in the heat of the moment." Instead, she suggests, write down all the emotions, take some time to review them dispassionately, and then form a rational response. "That way, you can think things through and decide whether or not it's even a battle worth fighting. If it is, you want to do it within twenty-four hours, but not within the first hour."

Taking the extra time also provides an opportunity to line up some allies, people to hold in reserve, in case things do not go as swimmingly as you hope. And when you do retaliate, do it with facts, rather than opinions, and in a style that keeps your emotions in check. Borrowing a line from *The Godfather*—"It's not personal; it's business"—

Browning cautions, "The reason you don't want to make it personal is because you might spend the rest of your career"—or if it happens outside of business, the rest of your life—"needing to interact with whoever attacked you."

While taking all of this into consideration, she acknowledges that when something happens that is off-the-charts egregious, an immediate, emotionally charged response might be exactly what's called for. However, she cautions, "You need to deploy that only after the most aggressive kind of attack."

Best Time to Get Pregnant Again

Ideally, anywhere from eighteen to fifty-nine months after delivering the previous child. A strict fifteen months used to be considered the optimal time to wait before conceiving again—the thinking here was that the first baby would be two years old, walking, and on his way to independence by the time the second one was born.

Dr. Elena Fuentes-Afflick, associate professor of epidemiology and biostatistics at the University of California, San Francisco, studied the behaviors and results of more than twenty-five thousand moms-to-be. She discovered that waiting from eighteen to fifty-nine months is preferable because "it makes a difference in terms of childhood mortality. There were higher instances of premature deliveries among women who got pregnant again without waiting at least eighteen months. We believe that this is due to nutritional factors and behavioral factors and the simple reality that it is emotionally stressful to have two children within a short period of time."

Waiting more than fifty-nine months presents its own set of problems, says Fuentes: "You get rusty. For reproductive purposes, your body goes into a certain rhythm. And once you fall out of that rhythm, it's hard to regain it."

Best Time to Get Drunk with a Client

When he's Japanese. "Among Japanese colleagues, an evening of liberal imbibing is often called for," says Roger E. Axtell, retired vice president of worldwide marketing for the Parker Pen Company and author of eight books on business etiquette. "Over in Japan, it's no sin to get drunk with clients. There is a lot of heavy drinking, and that is when your Japanese clients let loose to the point where you find out what they really think. However, the etiquette is that it's outwardly forgotten the next morning." If you're not comfortable with kamikaze alcohol consumption, you can beg off by insisting that you have a medical condition. However, Axtell says, "You will seem insincere if you don't drink with them." This might hurt your ability to do business.

Back in the United States—and most of the world—the hard-drinking custom is not exactly embraced. While a few social cocktails in celebration of closing a big deal are fine, Axtell insists, "I don't know that there would ever be a good time to get drunk with an American client. You don't want to lose control and risk saying something that will damage a business relationship." In the United States, unlike in Japan, everything is not forgotten the next morning.

⏰ *Bad Gifts* ⏰

It may not be as damaging as getting smashed and making a pass at a client's wife, but giving an inappropriate gift won't exactly get you into anyone's good graces, either. Here, courtesy of Roger E. Axtell, are the international equivalents of a bouquet of black roses.

China: Do not give a clock, certainly not to an older person, as it has a funeral connotation.

Japan: Four of anything in Japan is bad luck. The word for four, *shi,* is synonymous with death. Instead, make a good impression by giving eight of something.

Mexico: Yellow marigolds are the flowers that people traditionally place in front of loved ones' tombstones. Presenting them in a bouquet is tantamount to wishing death upon the recipient.

Brazil: Purple flowers have the same chilling effect as yellow marigolds in Mexico.

Germany, Switzerland, and Austria: Do not give your hostess a bouquet of roses—unless you plan on seducing her after dinner. *Rose* derives from the word *rosa,* which means "secret" in Latin. Presenting a bouquet of roses hints that you want to begin a clandestine affair.

Middle East: A box of handkerchiefs would be considered a downbeat gift (hankies are symbolic of crying), and if you pass it to somebody with your left hand, you are out-and-out insulting that person. The left hand is considered the unclean hand—a belief that goes beyond the symbolic in a region where bathrooms sometimes lack toilet paper but are outfitted with faucets conveniently placed to the left of the toilet. To digress a bit more, it explains why, if you really want to punish an Arab for stealing, you chop off his right hand, which leaves him outside of even the most marginally polite society.

Best Time to Mess with the Media

Middle of the week, late in the morning. So says Joey Skaggs, a thirty-nine-year veteran of fooling reporters and broadcasters into giving prime coverage to patently bogus services and products such as his "cathouse for dogs" and his cockroach-hormone pills, which supposedly cure everything from acne to menstrual cramps. "You can't do something on Sunday because it's a news-off day; nobody will bother coming to cover your press conference or event," says Skaggs. "And you need to do it in the morning so that you can make that day's news cycle"—especially if you want to get into the paper before reporters have a chance to realize they've been hoaxed. "Plus, you need to look at the calendar and see what else is coming up in the news, to make sure that nothing will overshadow you."

Skaggs perpetrates elaborate frauds, which often require dozens of extras to make them particularly believable. Such was the case with Fat Squad Commandos, in which he played Joe Bones, ex–U.S. Marine Corps drill sergeant, and led a platoon of toughies who supposedly beat and berated people into losing weight. "The Europeans loved that one; they love any story that makes Americans look fat and stupid," says Skaggs. "Media people are willing to be conned if you give them a good-enough visual and put on a good-enough performance."

His scams work even when people are expecting to be fooled: "Every April Fools' Day for the last nineteen years, I have gotten press outside of New York for an April Fools' Day Parade that didn't exist," boasts Skaggs.

Best Time to Come Out of the Closet

Summer. "People are in good moods, there's not a lot of stress, and there are no family holidays—which are terrible times for coming out," says Charles Purdy, etiquette columnist for *SF Weekly* and author of the book *Urban Etiquette*. "Plus, everybody gets a vacation in the summer, so it's a good time for you to take a week off from work and spend three days with your family, explaining what's going on in your life. Then you can use the rest of the time as part of a long weekend in Palm Springs."

In terms of your emotional state, Purdy believes that it's best to break the news before you fall in love—"It's easier to tell your parents you're gay than it is to tell them that you're moving in with somebody and bringing him home for Thanksgiving dinner"—and to do it in front of small groups of friends or family members. "You want them to be able to absorb the news without having to deal with one another's emotions on top of it. Some families react the same way they would if you announced that you were moving to a far-off state—a little sad, but really no big deal—while others practically go into mourning."

Best Time to Sue for Millions

After you suffer a catastrophic, life-altering injury and (this part is critical) it happens at the hands of a big, neglectful, heinous, and ultraprofitable company. "When corporations put the making of money over the safety of people, they pay significant penalties," says Andrew Finkelstein, managing partner at Jacoby & Meyers, the personal-injury law firm famous for its late-night commercials and toll-free phone numbers. "Juries are made up of people who want companies to act responsibly. Jurors react adversely when companies fail to do the right thing. And there are a lot of hateful companies out there. The ones you hear about just happen to be bad at hiding what they are."

Finkelstein has won hundreds of millions of dollars for clients—in one decision, for example, a negligent company paid in excess of twenty-eight million dollars—and he's miffed about the déclassé image that his firm has. "Everyone who says they hate lawyers should know that they could put me out of business instantly if companies would do the right thing," says Finkelstein, whose firm represents only clients who have broken bones and/or require surgery. If you've been emotionally abused, go somewhere else.

How bad does corporate irresponsibility get? "There is a saw manufacturer that can place a guard over its blade, but the guard is left off"—causing at least one person to lose an arm—"because employers want it that way so the workers can finish their jobs quicker," says Finkelstein. "One guy of mine had both of his arms burned off, due to an electrical box on a pole that was supposed to have no current running through it. Then there's the car manufacturer that won't put a twelve-dollar clamp on its automobile's shoulder harnesses—even though they know that it would prevent paraplegic injuries in collisions. It's cheaper to pay off the injured people."

Asked how his clients feel when they get the big bucks, Finkelstein somberly replies, "Every one of them would happily give up the money if that could make the injury go away."

Best Time to Approach a Celebrity

After he's finished eating dinner and is waiting for his car at the restaurant's valet stand. "He's had a few drinks, he's been fed, and he's looking good," says Giuliana DePandi, on-air host for E! Entertainment Television. "Another reason why a celebrity won't mind being approached while waiting for his car is because he can escape from you in two minutes. Walk up to the same person while he's sitting in a restaurant, eating, and he's afraid he'll be trapped with you for the rest of his meal."

Approaching a celebrity in a nightclub is not too bad—especially if you do it in the VIP room. DePandi figures that they're putting themselves out there when they're clubbing, so they can't expect too much privacy. "But," she suggests, "make eye contact first, flirt from a distance, and let them invite you over. If the celebrity thinks you're hot, he or she will invite you to sit down. However, if you're a guy, don't gaze too much, or you might get mistaken for a stalker. The most important thing of all is to be cool and to remember that guys like Vince Vaughn aren't looking for new best friends at the moment."

⊕ *Worst Times to Approach a Celebrity* ⊕

A lot of people do a lot of stupid things because they become weird or desperate or flustered when they are within touching distance of a movie star. Here are Giuliana DePandi's tips on when not to act any of those ways:

When he looks like the rest of us: "Celebrities in baseball caps and sunglasses, with a few days of stubble and disheveled hair, want to be left alone."

When he's shopping for groceries: "They don't want you looking in their carts and seeing something embarrassing."

When he's standing in line at Starbucks: "The celebrity hasn't had his coffee yet, so he's not going to be in a great mood. If he's sitting there alone drinking it, he's not looking for company."

When he's waiting for a doctor's appointment: "He is probably nervous and trying to seem anonymous."

When he's gambling in a casino: "If the guy is between hands, you say something to him, and he loses, he'll be convinced that you're unlucky. However, if the celebrity is *winning* in a casino, he's just gotten free money, so he's happy as can be, and that might be the greatest time of all to approach him."

Best Time to Buy Home Accessories

May, October, and just prior to Christmas. "That's when you get the opportunity to buy overstocks, discontinued lines, items that had been manufactured but never produced in large quantities, and things that didn't market well," says Bonnie Kurtz, owner of outletsonsale.com, a Web site that tracks opportunities to buy home accessories at reduced prices. "Those are the times of year when manufacturers clear out their inventory."

These blowouts are usually held in warehouses, tents, or showrooms. You can find out about them by scouring newspapers for ads or searching the Internet. "I paid fifteen dollars for bistro lamps at a sale being held by America Retold," recalls Kurtz. "Then, a few months later, I saw the exact same lights in a retail store for seventy-five dollars. Normally, at these sales, you can expect to pay wholesale or less. It's usually half of what the item will retail for, minus 10 to 20 percent."

Best Time to Retire

When you have enough money socked away that you can withdraw 4 percent from your portfolio each year, increasing (or decreasing) it by whatever percentage the previous year's rate of inflation (or deflation) had been. In other words, if you've got one million dollars, then you need to live on forty thousand dollars per year (with the inflation/deflation changes factored in).

Though the formulation was computed by a group of professors at Trinity University in San Antonio, Texas, it's spread like gospel by John P. Greaney, a former chemical engineer who retired at thirty-eight and advises others on how to do it via his Web site, retireearlyhomepage.com. "The study said that you need to have 75 percent of your holdings in stock and 25 percent in bonds," says Greaney, who was so hell-bent on retiring at a young age that he banked 50 percent of his take-home salary for three years before quitting his job in 1994. "By taking out only 4 percent per year, you will always have enough money to survive, even if there is a stock market crash like the one in 1929."

By the way, if you want to retire young, like Greaney did, and you don't make a ton of money (after taxes and savings, he lived on twenty thousand dollars per year from 1991 through 1994), he has a few suggestions: Live somewhere cheap (Greaney used to reside in Baton Rouge and is now in Houston), get married (two can, more or less, live for the price of one), and forget about anyone carrying on the family name. "One common element among people who retire young is that there are no children. Throw kids into the mix and things get tough."

Greaney acknowledges that colleagues thought he was crazy when he told them he was going to quit his job and retire at such a young age. "They asked me what I would do with myself," he recalls. "I told them that I hoped I wouldn't have to do a whole lot of anything. As it turns out, I play golf, watch TV, and sleep late."

Best Time to Close the Deal (with a Love Interest or a Sales Prospect)

Right from the start. "The first word that comes out of your mouth should move a prospect toward closing," says Ross Jeffries, the creator of a system called Speed Seduction, which is designed specifically for getting women into bed quickly but can also be applied to selling widgets. "I lead the other person to imagine that she's already committed to doing what I'm asking her to do, and to attach good feelings to it. Then I ask her to imagine what it would be like to have all the things we've been discussing. Once she does that, I close the deal."

Yeah, but what if she's imagining some repulsive scenario that no sensible person would want any part of? Like, uhm, getting into bed with Jeffries? Jeffries insists that he can sense this as well and knows how to abort the mission *tout de suite.* "If they're leaning forward and giving me their full attention, their facial muscles are smooth and their pupils are dilating, then they are in a buying trance and will agree to what I am suggesting. If I can't get somebody to that point, there's no reason to try closing the deal. Either I won't be able to do it or she'll get buyer's remorse. And there's no sense in that."

Best Time to Stage a Coup

Whether you're looking to take over a country, a company, or a conversation, conditions that create the best time for a coup are universal. "You want there to be a high misery index—people not getting their basic needs taken care of—a whiff of corruption, military grievances, and well-mobilized rebels," explains John A. Tures, who is presently an assistant professor at LaGrange College and who formerly worked on predicting coups for a Washington, D.C.–based think tank. "When those elements combine, you have a golden opportunity for somebody to step in and say that a change is required."

Tures adds that there are certain factors that reduce the likelihood of a coup: "Countries with foreign investments, international trade, and links with other nations around the world are less likely to have coups." What do you do when you sense a coup is in the offing? "Get ready to become flexible and choose the right side to jump onto."

Best Time to Be Liberal

When conservatives are in power. According to Mark Walsh, CEO of Air America, the liberal talk-radio network, "that's when you've got nowhere to go but up. It's the time for us to grow into roles of leadership and get organized." For Walsh, the fight seems to be as much fun as the victory, and he's intrigued by the process of repositioning the Democratic Party into a sharply defined machine: "As of mid-2004, we're out of power because we're bad at politics, and the Republicans' core strengths—defense and fiscal management—are what people care about."

Nevertheless, Walsh insists that those strengths are more a matter of perception than reality. "Democrats are getting better and meaner about pointing out inconsistencies between what Republicans promise and what they deliver," says Walsh, who has a megawatt bully pulpit from which to broadcast those views. "We're trying to show rational, centrist voters that Democrats are better at defense and fiscal issues than it may appear." Asked for proof, he quickly responds, "The biggest booms and smallest deficits occurred under Democratic presidents. And that can't be coincidental."

Best Time to Be Conservative

When liberals are in power. So says Richard Lessner, executive director at the American Conservative Union. "We're at our best when we face opposition," maintains Lessner. "We don't do government." In his mind, conservatives would rather go against the liberal grain—thus keeping the Democrats in check—than support a Republican president they might not completely agree with. When Republicans are in power, "we get torn between loyalties and principles. Besides, it's tough to beat up on your friends. It's always more fun to beat up on your enemies."

Told that Mark Walsh believes that the best time to be a liberal is when conservatives are calling the shots, Lessner cuts loose with a pretty good chuckle. Then he replies, "They've got that right. See, the liberals and conservatives have more in common than one might suspect."

ACKNOWLEDGMENTS

Thanks to the many, many experts who agreed to be interviewed and shared their opinions on the best times to do everything in this book. Additional appreciation goes out to magazine editors for whom some of this book's material originated: David Schonauer at *American Photo*; Sherri Burns and Jill Becker at *American Way*; Eric Wetzel at *Book*; Marvin Shanken, Gordon Mott, and Shandana Durrani at *Cigar Aficionado*; Pete Finch, Bob Sabat, Katrina Brown Hunt, Charlie Butler, and Nancy Smith at *SmartMoney*; and Sia Michel and Dave Itzkoff at *Spin*. Catherine Romano was my editor at *Reader's Digest,* where *The Best Time to Do Everything* first ran as a magazine piece.

Agents Kimberly Witherspooon and David Forrer, along with the entire Witherspoon Associates staff, did a great job of selling this book and handling countless details between then and now. Karen Rinaldi, Colin Dickerson, and Marisa Pagano at Bloomsbury provided sharp editorial advice and encouragement. Support, as always, came from my parents, Stan and Gladys, brother Ron, and sister Randi. Leonor Pena kept things magnificently together on the home front. And my family—Melodie, Lola, and Chloe—is simply the best.

INDEX

Best time to

Approach a celebrity 163

Argue your case 16

Ask for a raise 80

Be dragged through the gossip columns 131

Be conservative 170

Be liberal 169

Be photographed 40

Buy a house 103

Bowl a perfect game 51

Buy a new car 1

Buy appliances 115

Buy art 7

Buy caviar 50

Buy designer clothing 15

Buy fish 25

Buy fruit 32

Buy home accessories 165

Buy jewelry 58

Buy life insurance 109

Buy new technology 64

Buy shoes 5

Buy the arcade game of your youth 12

Buy tickets from a scalper 10

Buy your kid his first set of golf clubs 55

Buy your neighbor's house 85

Catch fish 83

Change 150

Cheat on your diet 20

Chuck it all and set sail 11

Clean up a murder scene 63

Close the deal 167

Come out of the closet 161

Cruise the Mediterranean 124

Deal with an obnoxious neighbor 143

Deal with the IRS 54

Deliver a baby 103

Do damage control 47

Do magic 82

Downsize 68

Drop a dime on someone 53

Enter the stock market 137

Fess up 47

Fight back 156

Find a tenant 122

Fire someone 39

Get a comfortable mammogram 35

Get a complimentary room upgrade at a hotel 77

Get a first kiss 2

Get a massage 66

Get an invention patented 127

Get comped at a casino 27

Get drunk with a client 158

Get married 95

Get pregnant 138

Get pregnant again 157

Get punched in the face 118

Get serious about wine 36

Get your car repaired 35

Get your name in the newspaper 76

Give bad news 145

Go into business with a spouse 34

Go pro in the kitchen 120

Go to the dentist 98

Go to the doctor 54

Go to the emergency room 23

Haggle 6

Have a Pap smear 143

Have a political debate 108

Have a punctual flight 22

Have a safe flight 74

Have an on-the-job romance 152

Have sex with 209 people in one session 123

Have surgery 72

Have your rich uncle die 147

Hire a landscaper 129

Launch a high-fashion modeling career 1

Launch a paradigm-shifting business 93

Lay low 21

Learn to play guitar 110

Listen to your body 141

Look for a job 132

Make a comeback 81

Make an outsize charitable donation 49

Mess with the media 160

Nail a tough restaurant reservation 78

Paint walls and refinish wooden floors 17

Pick up a lunch or dinner tab 155

Pick up somebody in a bar 107

Pig out with a high-cholesterol dinner 148

Place a sports bet 6

Plant a garden 139

Play basketball 91

Play over your head 96

Plead the Fifth 92

Pose nude for *Playboy* 30

Pose nude for *Playgirl* 146

Purge and organize 41

Put money into a retirement account 75

Raise capital 57

Raise your bet 88

Rattle an interview subject 31

Redecorate your living room 104

Refinance a mortgage 112

Renovate your home 125

Rent a car 70

Replace your home's roof and windows 62

Restructure debt 141

Retain information 60

Retire 166

Reveal a potentially disturbing fetish to your lover 65

Run into a burning building 44

See the Northern Lights 59

Seek a divorce 129

Sell a family business 114

Sell art and antiques 119

Sell your house 153

Serve jury duty 43

Sleep late 38

Snap a paparazzi picture 99

Stage a coup 168

Start a diet 44

Start a road trip 45

Stick with a job that you hate 117

Stop renting 128

Sue for millions 162

Sweat a perp 25

Take a catnap 134

Take a chance in business 14

Take a home pregnancy test 87

Take credit 151

Teach your dog a trick 3

Terminate psychotherapy 136

Thank your parents 27

Throw a knockout punch 71

Throw in the towel 133

Travel to the Caribbean 31

Visit Europe 91

Wait in line 101

Work late 86

Work out 11

Write a scathing tell-all about your famous boss 113

A NOTE ON THE AUTHOR

Michael Kaplan is a journalist based in Brooklyn, New York. His writing has appeared in such publications as *Wired, Details, Spin, Playboy,* and *SmartMoney.* He is the gambling columnist for *Cigar Aficionado.*

A NOTE ON THE TYPE

The text of this book is set in Linotype Sabon, named after the type founder Jacques Sabon. It was designed by Jan Tschichold and jointly developed by Linotype, Monotype, and Stempel, in response to a need for a typeface to be available in identical form for mechanical hot metal composition and hand composition using foundry type. Tschichold based his design for Sabon roman on a font engraved by Garamond, and Sabon italic on a font by Granjon. It was first used in 1966 and has proved an enduring modern classic.